AT WORK WITH GROTOWSKI
ON PHYSICAL ACTIONS

Published here in English for the first time, *At Work with Grotowski on Physical Actions* is a compelling account of nearly a decade's work of one of the central figures of twentieth-century theatre.

Jerzy Grotowski's closest collaborator, Thomas Richards, provides a thorough and compelling insider's view of the more recent period of Grotowski's research. He writes with clarity and passion of his apprenticeship with the master director. Grotowski himself contributes a preface and a major new essay "From the Theatre Company to Art as Vehicle." Not since the publication of Grotowski's own *Towards a Poor Theatre* (1968) has this profoundly influential theatre practitioner's work been so thoroughly or accurately explored.

Thomas Richards, a performing artist, earned a degree in Music and Theatre Studies from Yale University as an undergraduate and also holds a Master's Degree in Art, Music and Performance from the University of Bologna. He became Jerzy Grotowski's assistant in 1986, when the Workcenter of Jerzy Grotowski was founded in Pontedera, Italy, and is now Grotowski's essential collaborator.

AT WORK WITH GROTOWSKI ON PHYSICAL ACTIONS

Thomas Richards

With a preface and the essay
"From the Theatre Company to Art as
Vehicle" by Jerzy Grotowski

London and New York

First published 1995
by Routledge
11 New Fetter Lane, London EC4P 4EE

Simultaneously published in the USA and Canada
by Routledge
29 West 35th Street, New York, NY 10001

© 1993, 1995 Thomas Richards

Preface and "From the Theatre Company to Art as Vehicle" © 1993,
1995 Jerzy Grotowski

Typeset in Palatino by Florencetype Ltd, Stoodleigh, Devon
Printed and bound in Great Britain by
Mackays of Chatham PLC, Chatham, Kent

British Library Cataloguing in Publication Data

A catalogue record for this book is available from the British Library

Library of Congress Cataloguing in Publication Data
A catalogue record for this book has been requested

ISBN 0-415-12491-3 (hbk)
ISBN 0-415-12492-1 (pbk)

I would here like to express my gratitude to a dear friend, Michel A. Moos, whose intense efforts and cooperation in the final phase of redaction have contributed greatly to the completion of the present English version.

Thomas Richards
Pontedera, February 1994

To Fabrizio Cruciani

CONTENTS

PREFACE

I consider this book a precious report that permits one to assimilate some of those simple and basic principles which the self-taught at times come to know, yet only after years of groping and errors. The book furnishes information regarding "discoveries" which the actor can understand in practice, without having to start each time from zero. Thomas Richards has worked with me systematically since 1985. Today he is my essential collaborator in the research dedicated to Art as vehicle, in which I am now involved at the Workcenter of Jerzy Grotowski, in Pontedera, Italy.

In *At Work with Grotowski on Physical Actions*, Thomas Richards does not speak of our present work, that is Art as vehicle. The reader will find indications about this subject in my text, "From the Theatre Company to Art as Vehicle," published in appendix. Mr. Richards' book speaks about the first three years of our work together, dealing with "physical actions," a *necessary premise* for anyone active in the field of performing arts.

Thomas Richards was born in New York City in 1962. Before working with me he studied at Yale University where he obtained a degree in Music and Theatre Studies. In 1985, he participated as a member of the performance team in the Focused Research Program I directed at the University of California, Irvine. After one year, I proposed that he become my assistant and we transferred to Italy where, in 1986, the Workcenter of Jerzy Grotowski was founded at the Centro per la Sperimentazione e la Ricerca Teatrale in Pontedera. He has continued his personal research in close collaboration with me, and has assumed responsibility for directing one of the two programs at the Workcenter. At the same time, he has continued to pursue his university studies, and in 1992 received his M.A. from the Department of Art, Music, and Performance at the University of Bologna.

The nature of my work with Thomas Richards has the character of "transmission"; to transmit to him that to which I have arrived in my life: the *inner* aspect of the work. I use the word "transmission" in the traditional sense – in the course of an apprenticeship, through efforts and trials, the apprentice conquers the knowledge, practical and precise, from another person, his teacher. A period of real apprenticeship is long and I have worked with Thomas Richards for eight years now. At the outset, he was the *doer* (he who does, he who is doing in action) and I led him from the outside. With the passing of time, I asked him not only to act as *doer* but also to lead the work. As the leader of one of the two groups at the Workcenter, he conducted the practical daily work – it was he who became the teacher of the group – while I remained on hand and sometimes worked directly with the members of the group. But mainly I pointed out, when it was necessary, practical problems which Mr. Richards then resolved with them. During this period I also continued the individual work with him. This process still goes on today. Therefore my working relationship with Thomas Richards (in the course of the first three years described in this book and of the five years following dedicated to Art as vehicle) is one of "transmission," and for this reason I feel he is the right person to write about the work.

Mr. Richards' present book is of notable value for the young actor who wants to dedicate his life to the battle in art. It speaks of some indispensable elements of craft which, once learned, i.e., dominated in practice, can help one to exit from dilettantism. Herein the reader can obtain much information on how not to be stuck in practice. He will also find many "private" episodes narrated by someone who, at the moment in which he writes, has acquired the knowledge and authority to guide, develop, and complete, alone, the work with others. In each of these anecdotes he has hidden an alarm or an indication concerning that interior and personal discipline of which we cannot speak only in technical terms, but without which every vocation becomes suffocated and there is no possibility of either learning or technique.

Jerzy Grotowski
February 1993

P.S. Over the last ten years my research was supported by, among others, American contributions and grants. I would like to express my appreciation to the University of California, Irvine, to the National Endowment for the Arts, to the Rockefeller Foundation, to the International Centre for Theatre Creation, and to the MacArthur Foundation for awarding me with a Fellowship.

My gratitude goes also to the French Ministry of Culture and to the Académie Expérimentale des Théâtres, directed by Michelle Kokosowski, for the help I received.

I especially wish to thank Peter Brook.

It would have been hard to go through these years without the constant care, help, and friendship of Mercedes and André Gregory.

And finally a very special acknowledgment to those who have made possible the existence and the functioning of my Workcenter in Pontedera, Italy: the Centro per la Sperimentazione e la Ricerca Teatrale, its director Roberto Bacci, and Carla Pollastrelli.

J.G.

AT WORK WITH GROTOWSKI ON PHYSICAL ACTIONS

by Thomas Richards

STANISLAVSKI AND GROTOWSKI: THE CONNECTION

Artists who do not go forward go backward.

Konstantin Stanislavski

There is no standing still, only evolution or involution.

Jerzy Grotowski

For the last eight years I have worked continually with Jerzy Grotowski. The practical knowledge I have of "the craft," I gained from him.

Grotowski knows that to learn something means to conquer it in practice. One must learn through "doing" and not through memorization of ideas and theories. Theories were used in our work only when they might help solve a practical problem at hand. The work with Grotowski was nothing like a school where one learns lessons by rote. I am convinced he was trying to teach not just my mind, but the whole of my being. Often he would repeat to me that the true apprentice knows how to steal, how to be a "good thief": this demands an active effort from the learner, because he should steal the knowledge trying to conquer the capacity *to do*.

Grotowski would often give me a specific task; for example, to resolve with our group some technical problem which had appeared in the work. If I asked Grotowski how to resolve this problem, there would normally come no reply or just a knowing smile. At that moment, I knew I had to figure it out for myself. Only when I had accomplished the task to the best of my ability, would he step in and analyze my mistakes. Then the process would begin again. This method of teaching takes an enormous amount of time and patience. The person learning will inevitably arrive at moments of failure. Such "failures" are

3

absolutely essential; for here, the apprentice begins to see clearly how to proceed along the right climb. Given that the way in which I learned to work with physical actions was not at all customary from the point of view of the current educational system, I do not here develop a theoretical analysis. Rather, I remember the way in which my comprehension of, and capacity to work with physical actions evolved through practical research with my teacher, Jerzy Grotowski.

I am aware that many people have experienced "Grotowski workshops" conducted by someone who studied with Grotowski in a session of five days, for example, twenty-five years ago. Such "instructors," of course, often pass on grave errors and misunderstandings. Grotowski's research might be mistakenly construed as something wild and structureless, where people throw themselves on the floor, scream a lot, and have pseudo-cathartic experiences. Grotowski's connection to tradition, and his link to Stanislavski, run the risk of being completely forgotten or not taken into account. Grotowski himself, however, did not forget those who came before him. Faced with his predecessors, he was a "good thief," examining thoroughly their techniques, analyzing critically their value, and stealing what might work for himself. Grotowski's work in no way negates the past but rather, searches in it for the useful tools that may help him in *his* work. "Create your own method. Don't depend slavishly on mine. Make up something that will work for you!"[1] These are the words of Stanislavski and this is exactly what Grotowski did.

The axis of this text is a method, or better yet, a practice, finally central to the work of Stanislavski, and later developed by Grotowski: *physical actions*. In the last ten years of his life, Stanislavski placed a new emphasis on what he called "physical actions." He stated a clear opinion of what he considered to be the core of his research: *"The method of physical actions is the result of my whole life's work."*[2] This strong statement calls for clear understanding. What did Stanislavski mean by "method of physical actions"? Why was he using the word "physical" instead of "psycho-physical"? Why, at the end of his life, was he speaking about "physical actions," when so much of his earlier research had been based on the attempt at calling forth precise emotions? And this work on physical actions, how does one put it into practice?

4

Grotowski is convinced that Stanislavski's most precious pearl is his final period of work, where the "method of physical actions" appeared. Why does Grotowski consider this method to be Stanislavski's most useful discovery? How did I learn from Grotowski to work with physical actions? These are some of the questions I touch upon in the present text. In order to translate into writing my understanding of the work on physical actions – a capacity nurtured in practice – I retrace some stages of my work with Grotowski, seeing the way in which he transmitted this capacity to me. In recalling the way I discovered the elements of this technique, I reflect upon the presence of these elements in the final period of Stanislavski's work; thus emphasizing a point which seems to me often overlooked: the tight connection which exists between Grotowski's work and the work that Stanislavski conducted in the final period of his life.

Jerzy Grotowski and Konstantin Stanislavski both dedicated their lives to research on *craft*. They worked with extraordinary stamina and persistence of personal effort, arriving at great achievements and discoveries in their art. Yet their respective processes of work are often greatly misunderstood. Why?

We live in an epoch in which our inner lives are dominated by the discursive mind. This fraction of the mind divides, sections off, labels – it packages the world and wraps it up as "understood." It is the machine in us that reduces the mysterious object which sways and undulates into simply "a tree." Since this part of the mind has the upper hand in our inner formation, as we age, life loses its taste. We experience more and more generally, no longer perceiving "things" directly, as a child, but rather as signs in a catalogue already familiar to us. The "unknown," thus narrowed and petrified, is turned into the "known." A filter stands between the individual and life. Such as it is, the discursive mind has difficulty tolerating an alive process of development. Like a small dog trying to hold a river by grasping it between its jaws, this mind labels the things around us, and claims: "I understand." Through such "understanding" we misunderstand, and reduce that which is being perceived to the limits and characteristics of the discursive mind. Such misunderstanding often occurs when we study the work of another person. The danger is that we limit, reduce, and cage

5

that person, seeing only what we wish to, or are able to see. At the outset, I should like to state that for me Stanislavski and Grotowski are like that raging river. I shall try my best not to be like a small dog faced with them and their life's work.

Turning toward the life of Stanislavski and that of Grotowski I see two truly alive processes; I see that their researches, through personal efforts, are like parabolas constantly in ascent. For this, it seems to me fundamental to study the final portion of their work. For here, we are able to see each man's personal perspective on his research, the respective conclusions arrived at, and what each one felt to be the most important elements of his work.

As a young acting student in the State Theatre Institute in Poland, Grotowski saw that "some part of the educational process was a waste of time." As a result, together with other acting students, he met and worked in a type of student's studio within the Theatre Institute, where he made independent research into the work of Stanislavski. When speaking to me about this period, Grotowski stressed that the professors of the Institute were not against this "school" within a school: on the contrary, they supported him. He said that from this independent practical research he learned to work with physical actions. In that moment he discovered, "Ah, there is something there, in the work of Stanislavski, some tool which can be of use." In his essay, "Risposta a Stanislavskij" ("Answer to Stanislavski"), Grotowski states:

> "When I was a student in the school of dramatic arts, in the faculty for actors, I founded the entire base of my theatrical knowledge on the principles of Stanislavski. As an actor, I was possessed by Stanislavski. I was a fanatic. I retained that it was the key that opens all the doors of creativity. I worked a lot to arrive to know all possible about that which he said or what was said about him."[3]

Despite the fact that Grotowski, in almost all of his public conferences, stresses the connection of his work to that of Stanislavski, I repeatedly see actors and theatre groups who in practice forget this point. They attempt to arrive at that same high quality, bounding over all need for essential fundamentals; they make a direct leap into the unknown. Through laziness or a desire for immediate results, such individuals or groups completely forget the teachings of Stanislavski which stress the need for a consciously prepared structure, a need which Grotowski never forgot.

> "Sure, the whirlwind of inspiration can carry our 'creative airplane' above the clouds [. . .] without running down the runway. The trouble is that these flights do not depend on us and do not constitute the norm. It is within our possibilities to prepare the ground, to lay the rails, that is to say to create the physical actions reinforced by truth and conviction."[4]

These are the words of Stanislavski, but many times I have heard Grotowski express the same idea.

It is very easy to dream of doing something profound. It is much more difficult to actually do something profound. An old Russian proverb says, If you go to your porch, look up at the sky, and jump to the stars, you will just land in the mud. Often the *stairs* are forgotten. The stairs *must be constructed*. This, Grotowski never forgot. One can easily get lost thinking about the profound metaphysical side of Grotowski's work, and forget completely the sacrifice and practical labor behind his results. But Grotowski first of all was a master *theatre director*.

As a young actor, I had no idea of the amount of mastery needed in the craft. That's why, now, I wish to stress that stairs are needed. This is our technique as artists and no matter how creative we feel ourselves to be, we have no channel for our creative force without technique. Technique means craftsmanship, a technical knowledge of our craft. The stronger your creativity is, the stronger your craft must be, in order to arrive at the needed equilibrium which will let your resources flow fully. If we lack this ground level, we surely land in the mud.

My hope is that, also by means of this text, the work on physical actions may find a greater practical use among theatre groups who seek to improve the quality of their work. I wish that they continually ask themselves what they can serve with their craft, other than vanity and purse, so that they might in their own hearts be able to call themselves "artists."

For what does one work? To be a saleable item? What does one *serve* with one's work?

Posing this question has paramount importance for both Stanislavski and Grotowski. "To serve" is foremost in their way of approaching art and the creative act. The accomplishment of one's work should serve something other than one's vanity or pride. Stanislavski said: "We must love not ourself in art, but art in ourself."[5] Probably everyone, to differing degrees, feels a need to serve something higher or more noble with their work. But certain persons, through their own persistent efforts, turn this feeling into action. They do not "stand still," but pursue a continual fight for personal growth, never succumbing to stagnation. Conscious growth does not occur accidentally or by itself. These persons work constantly and through their efforts attempt to serve something over themselves. Such persons often arrive at great discoveries, and also are often greatly misunderstood.

This text tells of the *first part* of my work with Jerzy Grotowski: the first three years of apprenticeship in which the work on physical actions was fundamental.

The period which follows constitutes a completely new stage and is not the topic of this text. The present work conducted by Grotowski – in which I am collaborating – is centered on structured actions based on ancient vibratory songs. Grotowski speaks of this in the essay published at the end of this book.

RYSZARD CIESLAK
AT YALE

I first encountered the working methods of Jerzy Grotowski through Ryszard Cieslak, a founding member of Grotowski's Laboratory Theatre of Wroclaw. Cieslak, who died in the summer of 1990, is world-renowned for his creation of the title role in Grotowski's production, *The Constant Prince*. Though I remember Cieslak saying, "I am not Grotowski," his connection to the work of Grotowski is clear: Cieslak's formation as an actor evolved in the Laboratory Theatre, where he became the leading actor during the group's highest creative period.

In my final year as an undergraduate at Yale University (1984), Ryszard Cieslak came to do a two-week workshop in the Theatre Studies Department. This workshop created in me an inner explosion. I had been sitting in university lectures for four years with experts talking at my head. My physicality completely blocked, I feared I was becoming a stuffed talking box and dreaded unconsciously that something inside me was dying. I immediately took to the physical thrust of Cieslak's work: it was fresh and alive, something for which I was starved. We did many improvisations. This work opened in me something which had been tightly shut after sitting for so long. It introduced me to a physical way of expression; I began to see the importance of the body for the actor.

After each session with Cieslak, I would practically run home dancing in the streets, such was the state of my excitement. I distinctly remember the impression of the street lamps reflecting light through the flakes of nighttime snow as I danced home.

When Cieslak came for the first time to our acting class, a normal scene study class, I had just read Grotowski's *Towards a Poor Theatre*. The ideas, methods of work, and ethics that I found

9

in this book, impressed me greatly. At the time, I did not really understand what Grotowski had said – I attributed this lack of understanding to the translation which I felt might have lost something of the original. I was greatly impressed, however, by the quality of the Laboratory Theatre's performances which I could sense almost physically jumping off the photographs in the book: each photograph captured and held me with some sort of visceral attraction.

When I heard it was Cieslak coming to do a workshop with us, and not Grotowski, I felt disappointed and cheated. I thought Cieslak must be second best, and that we Yale students deserved better.

Our acting class was in full swing when Cieslak walked in. I practically fell out of my chair, I had never felt such presence from anyone. "My God, this is a dinosaur, people like this don't exist any more. He walks like a tiger." Cieslak sat down and with his presence alone he began to take over and dominate our class. Faced with him I felt like a docile schoolboy, a well-trained circus animal next to a wild panther. Through his presence alone, and almost completely silently, he stripped our acting teacher of his authority. Shortly thereafter he would be demanding our acting teacher to "Tell us what Chekhov is to you? What is he to *you?*" A mini-revolution took place, I was spellbound. Our acting teacher, a very proud man, completely stunned, turned over our class to Cieslak and left the room. We were alone with him.

The work with Cieslak was an eye and body opening period: a taste of some other possibility which had a deep effect on my unconscious. I started having many wild and colorful dreams. For example, I dreamed we were working and the room caught on fire. We had to jump out of the windows to escape, but I was not afraid of the fire.

Cieslak worked directly, with no fear. I immediately and almost instinctively admired these qualities in him. I think some of the other students became frightened by his direct approach. Once, he asked if someone wanted to work on vocal technique. At first no one raised a hand out of shyness, but after some time a girl known to have a high squeaky voice volunteered; he asked her if she knew some text by heart and as she spoke this text, he tried to help her discover a deeper vocal resonator. After many strategies had failed, he was even holding her around the groin area from behind bouncing her up and down. I think some of the students were shocked by this method, but I never felt uneasy. There was nothing low or demeaning about it. It seemed actually very organic, like two bears playing. He also had her sing balancing on her hands, feet in the air leaning against the wall. These ways of doing – direct, physical, and demanding – shocked us Yale undergraduates, accustomed to a lot of talk and discussion. Cieslak would drive an actor straight to his own personal limits, at the same time emanating a powerful warmth.

I remember once he said that the human voice can go incredibly high. He asked if we had ever heard the highest note of the Chinese scale and if someone would like to discover this. I volunteered. I spoke a text I knew by heart trying to use a very high resonator in the head. I guess it was not working because he asked me to repeat the word "King-King" and go higher and higher in register. All the time he was saying, almost shouting, "Higher!" hitting me very sharply on the spot on my head where I thought the sound should come out. His hand swung in a very fast downward motion. The force of the blow did not strike directly on my head, but more across my skull, like a slice, about two inches back from the top of the cranium. Although the contact made a loud sound, I was not hurt. The actual resonator he indicated is near the point where his hand met my skull (the place of this vocal resonator can be clearly seen in *Towards a Poor Theatre*, on page 179).[6] After that exercise he had me sit against the wall to rest without speaking for fifteen minutes. I suppose I needed to repose my vocal cords, which were not used to that type of direct work. In this moment, when he walked me to the wall, I have no words to explain the warmth I felt from him: it had such a strong human quality. The sensation of that warmth, combined with the fact that I had tried to do something really unknown – not just with my mind but also with other parts of myself – led me to feel an incredible trust in him. Cieslak was like that. If you were willing, he would push you very warmly straight to your limits.

One day he proposed that we students prepare an improvisation alone, and show it to him the next day. Before he left, he told us we must make a preliminary outline for the improvisation: *we should not improvise without a structure,* but *pre-construct* the basic outline. This would give us points of reference, like telegraph poles, which he called "repairs"; without this structure we would be lost. Then he left us by ourselves to work.

11

We invented the story of a wedding involving everyone in the class. We discussed our characters, their relations to one another, and created an outline for the improvisation. The next day, however, when we did the improvisation with Cieslak watching, someone broke the structure. Total chaos ensued. We had no channel for our stream: we were completely lost.

Cieslak then tried to make us aware of the amount of work involved in creating a performance starting from improvisations. He said if we wanted to turn that improvisation into a performance, each of us should take his notebook, divide each page into two columns, and write in one column, as precisely as possible, absolutely everything that he had *done* during the improvisation; and in the other column, write everything that he had *associated* inwardly: all physical sensations, mental images and thoughts, memories of places, people. I understood when Cieslak spoke about "associations" that he meant: While you are doing your actions, in the same moment your mind's eye is seeing something, as if a memory flashes before you. He said that, through all this which we had written down, we would be able to reconstruct, memorize and repeat the improvisation we had just done. Then, we could work on the structure, altering and perfecting it until it had become a performance.

This was the only time in the workshop that Cieslak spoke about the discipline involved in the actor's craft, a discipline which he himself had clearly mastered. He never *spoke* about physical actions. I don't think Cieslak concerned himself with teaching us craft: he had very little time with us. It seemed, rather, that he sensed in us some grave limitations – inner limitations – and tried to help unearth in those of us who wished, some new aspect or possibility. If this was his intention, he achieved it fully. I suppose this work can be accused of not making technical demands on us, thus reinforcing a kind of dilettantism already present; but I think his intention was different: to give us a glimpse of something very precious that we clearly lacked.

I remember Cieslak one day saying an actor must be able to cry like a child, and he asked if one of us could do it. A girl lay down on the floor and tried. He said, "No, not like that," and taking her place on the floor, transformed himself into a crying child before our eyes. Only now, after many years, do I understand the key to Cieslak's success in this transformation.

12

He found the *exact physicality* of the child, its alive physical process which supported his child-like scream. He did not look for the child's emotional state, rather with his body he remembered the child's physical actions. Stanislavski is quoted as saying, "Do not speak to me about feeling. We cannot set feeling; we can only set physical action."[7] At that time, however, I did not understand the process behind Cieslak's transformation. I had just seen a master actor at work. What he had done was amazing to watch, but I had no idea how to achieve such a result myself. Impressed, I was left longing to be able to do something, without the knowledge of how to do it.

Near the end of the workshop, Cieslak spent a long time on an "étude" with one boy. I saw Cieslak had a vast technical knowledge of the actor's craft. The boy was to remember the face of his girlfriend before him. Without an actual partner, he had to recreate his way of touching her face, as if she were really there and they were alone. For the actor, only she, his invisible partner, should exist; not us, the spectators. Each time the young actor attempted this action he could not find a sense of truth. He "acted," trying to show us how much he cared for her. What came out was forced, not believable. Cieslak demanded that he repeat again and again, as if saying, "No, don't concentrate on the feelings. What did you do?" Cieslak directed the boy's attention to the physical details: "Don't act. What was the touch of her skin like? At what moment precisely do you touch your girlfriend's face? Is her face warm or cold? How does she react to your touch? How do you react to her reaction?" Despite Cieslak's unflagging efforts, the young actor did not arrive *with his body* at the true remembering. When he arrived at his most truthful moment, however, Cieslak immediately stopped him, evidently so that he might have as last impression his most truthful moment.

As I look back, I see this was my first insight into Stanislavski's "method of physical actions." Compared to the other work with Cieslak, this "étude" seemed normal, too normal for my young body that ached for adventure. I was not yet ready to appreciate the painstakingly precise work needed to master a craft. With Grotowski later, however, I found out that the work on physical actions is exactly this extremely painstaking way, in which nothing can be done "in general."

"'*In general*,' said Stanislavski, 'is the enemy of art.'"[8]

All this Cieslak knew from experience. Often he would do demonstrations that left our mouths open in astonishment. But the same question remained: "How did he do that?" The rest of his work had not made technical demands on us, as that one "étude" with the young actor had done; so, I did not then receive a practical answer.

We did, however, begin to rediscover how to romp, as kids do. We were all young, but something in us had already become stiff, not just physically, but psychologically as well. We were already carrying many fears. Maybe this is what Cieslak had sensed and was trying to attack in his workshop. He seemed much younger than us though he was already forty-seven. I'm not sure what was so young in Cieslak, but there was something light in his eyes and around him. Despite his age, he had this something and we did not; from this "something" his youth came. Once, when we were sluggish in a series of physical exercises, he urged us on saying, "You are all young! Look at you! And me, I'm old." And with the confidence of a cat he hopped onto his head, balanced on one shoulder, and then bounced back onto his feet. We were all amazed by his agility and especially by his lack of hesitation. Had he asked anyone of us to do the same, there would have followed at least five seconds of hesitation as the candidate thought about how to do it. But in him there was no hesitation, his body was thinking in the process of doing.

This workshop left me in some confusion. I saw that a very deep possibility existed in myself and in theatre, but I was still an amateur as before. I did not have the technique or knowledge to arrive at any level.

Six years later, at the Homage to Ryszard Cieslak after his death, Grotowski spoke about Cieslak in *The Constant Prince*:

"When I think of Ryszard Cieslak, I think of a *creative* actor. It seems to me that he was really the incarnation of an actor who plays as a poet writes, or as Van Gogh was painting. We can't say that he is somebody who played imposed roles, already structured characters, at least from a literary point of view, because, even if he kept the rigor of the written text, he created a quality entirely new. [. . .]

It is very rare that a symbiosis between a so-called director and a so-called actor can go beyond all the limits of the technique, of a philosophy, or of ordinary habits. This arrived to such a depth that often it was difficult to know if there were two human beings working, or a double human being. [. . .]

Now I am going to touch on a point which was a particularity of Ryszard. It was necessary not to push him and not to frighten him. Like a wild animal, when he lost his fear, his closure we can say, his shame of being seen, he could progress months and months with an opening and a complete liberation, a liberation from all that in life, and even more in the work of the actor, blocks us. This opening was like an extraordinary trust. And when he could work in this way for months and months with the director alone, after he could be in the presence of his colleagues, the other actors, and after even in the presence of the spectators; he had already entered into a structure which assured him, through rigor, a security.

Why do I think that he was an actor as great as, in another field of art, Van Gogh for example? Because he knew how to find the connection of gift and rigor. When he had a score of acting, he could keep to it in the most minute details. This – it is the rigor. But there was something mysterious behind this rigor which appeared always in connection with trust. It was the gift, gift of self – in this sense, the gift. Attention! It was not the gift to the public! No. It was the gift to something much higher, which overpasses us, which is above us and also, we can say, it was the gift to his work, or it was the gift to our work, the gift to us both. [. . .]

The text speaks of tortures, of pains, of an agony. The text speaks of a martyr who refuses to submit to the laws which he does not accept. [. . .] But in working as director with Ryszard Cieslak, we never touched anything which was sad. The whole role was based on a very precise time from his personal memory linked to the period in which he was an adolescent and had his first big, extraordinary amorous experience. All was linked to that experience. This referred to that kind of love which, as it can only arrive in adolescence, carries all its sensuality, all that which is carnal, but, in the same time, behind that, something totally different that is not carnal, or which is carnal in another way, and which is much more like a prayer. It's

15

as if, between these two sides, appears a bridge which is a carnal prayer. [. . .]

And even during months and years of preparatory work, even when we were alone in this work, without the other members of the group, one can't say that this was an improvisation. This was a return to the most subtle impulses of the lived experience, not simply to recreate it, but to take flight toward that impossible prayer. But yes, all the little impulses and all that which Stanislavski would call physical actions (even if, in his interpretation, it would be much more in another context, the one of social game, and here it was not at all that) – even if everything was like refound, the true secret was to go out of the fear, of the refusal of himself, to go out of that, to enter into a big free space where he could have no fear at all and hide nothing. [. . .]

The first step toward this work was that Ryszard dominated totally the text. He learned the text by heart, he absorbed it in such a way that he could start in the middle of a phrase of any fragment, still respecting the syntax. And at this point, the first thing we did was to create the conditions in which he could, as literally as possible, put this flow of words on the river of the memory, of the memory of the impulses of his body, of the memory of the small actions, and with the two take flight, take flight, like in his first experience: I say first in the sense of his base experience. That base experience was luminous in an indescribable way. And with that luminous thing, put in montage with the text, with the costume which makes reference to Christ or with the surrounding iconographic compositions which also allude to Christ, there appeared the story of a martyr, but we never worked with Ryszard starting from a martyr, all to the contrary. [. . .]

We can say that I demanded from him everything, a courage in a certain way inhuman, but I never asked him to produce an effect. He needed five months more? Okay. Ten months more? Okay. Fifteen months more? Okay. We just worked slowly. And after this symbiosis, he had a kind of total security in the work, he had no fear, and we saw that everything was possible because there was no fear."[9]

16

As soon as Cieslak left my university, I thought: "I have to find Grotowski," the source of Cieslak's mastery. I went to look for scholarships to Poland, but all of them required that I speak Polish. A few weeks later, I was stunned when the director of our Theatre Studies Department announced that Grotowski himself was going to arrive. He was coming to make a selection of Yale students who would work for two weeks that summer, in his Objective Drama Program at the University of California, Irvine. He had emigrated from Poland two years before. When Grotowski arrived at Yale, I passed the selection and, that summer (1984), with eleven other students left for California.

Before we left, I remember the director of Theatre Studies saying that from his conversations with Grotowski during the selection period, he understood that somehow when Grotowski worked with an actor, it was as if Grotowski lived through that actor. Our director stressed that should this happen to one of us during the workshop, we should not hesitate or resist. He encouraged us on our way.

THE WORKSHOP
AT THE OBJECTIVE DRAMA
PROGRAM

Working with Grotowski for two weeks in California, I began to understand the meaning of *improvisation within a structure*.

At Yale University, as a musician I often improvised, having already studied saxophone and clarinet for seven years. With a music professor and a few other musicians, we formed a free improvisation music ensemble. Our improvisations had no structure and could never be repeated: musical competence and our ability to listen and react sonically were the only structural elements. At Irvine, however, Grotowski strongly emphasized the need for structure when one improvises. Many times when speaking about improvisation, he gave the example of early jazz. He said early jazz musicians understood improvisation could exist only within a definite structure: they had mastered their instruments, and were starting from a base melody. Their improvisations were woven starting from that melody, which was their structure, and with which they were always keeping in relation. Whenever giving this example, Grotowski stressed he was speaking about *early* jazz.

The day before the workshop began, Grotowski came to our dorm to speak to us. I remember him saying that the next day we should present to him and his team of four assistants, "something." We should create a presentation based on what we thought the work with him was going to be. Perhaps some of us had had daydreams about the work. We should create this "something" around what we had imagined, what we had dreamed the work with him might be. Grotowski left us to prepare, but we were not sure how to begin. We had arrived expecting him to tell us what to do; we were ready to be passive and go along. He surprised us by asking us to be active. We decided

19

to do an improvisation: each of us would think up one section for the improvisation, and lead the others in it the following day. It took only a few minutes for us to come up with our individual propositions, so we spent the rest of the day at the beach.

The next day we showed up at Grotowski's workspace to do our presentation. While improvising, I thought we were achieving something quite intense. We huddled in a group and invented a song, we spontaneously created ritualistic dances, we went outside (the workspace was on the edge of the desert) and beat sticks in the sign of the cross facing the sun, all the while doing some improvised chanting. Feeling pretty primal, we ran into the desert without our shoes on. The sharp desert shrubbery cut up our feet. Grotowski then interrupted our improvisation and asked if we had all recently had tetanus shots. Three of us who had not were sent to the hospital to have our shots renewed.

Despite the confused ending to our improvisation, afterward I felt drained and happy with myself. Even my wounded feet did not bother me so much: they merely added to my conviction that we had "really done something."

In his analysis, Grotowski shocked our entire group by thanking us for showing him all the clichés of "paratheatrics" (or "participatory theatre"). He said in "paratheatrics" certain clichés inevitably appear, and he was astounded that they had appeared in the presentation of we young students who had not yet been exposed to such work and learned these clichés from others. Thus it was possible for him to see that such clichés were universal human banalities, not just limited to certain groups of people involved in this type of work. Grotowski made a list: to carry someone in the air as if he is dead; to throw yourself down on the ground in a pseudo-crisis; to scream; to herd up in a close bunch, singing improvised songs with syllables like "Ah ah" or "La la"; etc. He said that often, before any real work could begin, a human being would have to vomit out all these banalities. Therefore, in our work with him, we should just from the very beginning make a list of such banalities, and absolutely avoid them: our improvisation had served as a perfect lesson for us to see exactly what we should *not do* in our work with him.

Although Grotowski's assistants came from several different countries, the workshop centered on certain traditional Haitian

songs; regarding their melodies we were allowed no improvisations. Once, while learning a song, one of our group
members, a musician, began to improvise a countermelody.
Here, Maud Robart, the Haitian woman leading the song,
abruptly stopped, and told him forcefully, *"no improvisation."*

We spent many days just learning the melodies. Then we
had to learn to sing in rhythm and make the room resonate with
our voices in a specific way. These elements we practiced
many hours a day. We also worked on two dances that would
accompany the songs. Tiga (Jean-Claude Garoute) and Maud,
the Haitian assistants of Grotowski, immediately confronted us
with the rigors of the performative craft. Before we ever had
an opportunity to improvise, we had already thoroughly
memorized and absorbed the songs. Improvisation meant we
would keep the specific song and dance without alteration,
improvising only our displacement in the space and the contact
between persons. Often, however, even these elements were
indicated by the assistants who led the improvisation. Thus,
structure was strongly present.

At the time, I was unaware that I was witnessing the two
aspects so important to the creative process in theatre, the two
poles that give a performance its balance and fullness: form
on one side, and stream of life on the other, the two banks of
the river that permit the river to flow smoothly. Without these
banks there will be only a flood, a swamp. This is the paradox
of the acting craft: only from the fight between these two
opposing forces can the balance of scenic life appear.

| Precision/Form | Stream of life |

This workshop with Grotowski emphasized the need for a
structure when improvising, a structure tightly controlled.
Always when we did an improvisation with the Haitian songs,
there was a leader, or a team of leaders, that we students should
closely follow.

I cannot say that I was trained technically in that first workshop with Grotowski. There was not enough time. But I did have another taste of something very deep, and, as after the workshop with Cieslak, I felt quite confused. The songs had such a strong effect on me; they continued to live singing in me long after the work had finished, even through my sleep. Often after work some of us would go to a restaurant called Bob's Big Boy. One night we arrived, sat down and started giving each other strange looks. Suddenly we began uncontrollably laughing: this spontaneous laughter lasted for quite some time. It turned out that we had all simultaneously had the same impulse, to leap over the counter and attack the cook. Also, the quality of my sleep had changed. I sometimes woke up in the middle of the night to find myself swimming in the bed like a fish; or I dreamed for example, that I was running in the desert and as I jumped in the air to avoid falling into a hole, I woke up with a sudden start because my body in bed had also jumped with the same impulse as in the dream. My dreams were becoming more vivid and colorful.

One point of extreme interest for me personally, which I noted during this workshop, concerns the quality of Grotowski's presence. When he was in the workspace I felt a considerable change in the space itself. This I cannot explain with words. I thought maybe I was simply nervous, he being a famous man. But no. I could always sense when he was looking at me, as if his eyes were touching.

One day we did an improvisation. Grotowski told us that encoded in each ancient song is a way of moving, *only one way*: each song contains, hidden inside itself, its own distinct way to move. Some of Grotowski's assistants would sing, repeating a predetermined cycle of Haitian songs, while the other assistants would accompany on the drums. Every student should search for the dance "encoded" in each song; they should, with their body, look to rediscover the way of moving in each song while the assistants sang and repeated the song cycle.

At first my mind was conducting the search for the dances, I was mentally interpreting the songs. About one of them, I deduced for example, that it must be a work song, so I imitated manual work, turning these movements into a repetitive dance. Well, we danced for a long time, it seemed we must have been going for some hours, nonstop. After a certain point, as my physical exhaustion grew, my mind became tired and quiet: it was less able to tell my body how to interpret the song. Then for some short moments I felt as if my body started to dance by itself. The *body* led the way to move, the mind became passive. I felt Grotowski's eyes on me, a clear impression, a physical sensation as if being touched. Then Grotowski abruptly ended the improvisation. As we walked out of the workspace he approached me and said, "Yes, that was in the right direction."

In that moment – when he said this – I cannot describe the weight contained behind his words. It was not just that I had received a compliment. I had received compliments before in my life, enough to make me full of myself and what I thought of as my talent. What struck me like a blow from Grotowski at that instant, was the exact thing for which I don't have words, which I tried to describe before as having to do with presence. I can only describe it now as a very warm weight. This led me to have an incredible sense of pride, a pride I had not before experienced. It was not petty, of vanity, but different, maybe of accomplishment. The weight and warmth behind the words of Grotowski, and not the words themselves, had left in me this strong impression.

The last night of the workshop, each of us had a chance to speak with Grotowski alone. When I spoke with him he said my work there had been good, and he asked what I would do next. I told him I would go back to New York to finish a performance on which I had started work.

I felt very confident in my potential as an actor, and now Grotowski's saying I had done well in his workshop, in my mind confirmed this. Ever since I was young I had the naïve notion that learning finished after college. Then life would be simply a breeze. At some moment I would get married, have children, be a star and famous, probably win a Tony award. All this seemed ordinary and natural.

Thus, full of myself, I was ready to go back to New York and become a profound actor, ready to shock the world from the depths of my soul. I felt convinced there was something very deep in myself and I was quite ready to "express it." What I saw as my success in Grotowski's workshop merely confirmed this.

IN NEW YORK

I got a job as a waiter to support myself financially while I entered rehearsals with a young theatre group. We prepared a classical tragedy, all committing to a long rehearsal period. Each person in the group was in his own way a follower or a great admirer of Grotowski. We worked for profound results, sparing no effort, and tried to create a physical form of expression. Serious, even super-serious, we loved to get together after rehearsal and belittle the normal banal theatre world; laughing and poking fun at those we considered trivial.

We rehearsed for nine months. During the part of the rehearsal period dedicated to improvisations, we all thought we were coming up with an extremely alive performance, and at that point something was extremely alive. But soon, however, there came the need to *structure and set* the elements in order to create the story. The date for performance was approaching. Here we ran into trouble: we fixed the physical line *in movements, not in actions.* I fixed my physical movements like a dance, but not even as precise as real choreography.

We were also interested in "facial mask" as spoken of by Grotowski in *Towards a Poor Theatre*, so for each of my characters I developed a set "mask" constructed by my face muscles. I understood much later that our way of elaborating this element was in practice a total misunderstanding of what Grotowski actually meant.

Many years later, Grotowski spoke to me about the facial masks his actors had used in *Akropolis*, and how they had arrived at them. The facial masks in *Akropolis* were not frozen, constructed for some formal reason, but rather directly linked to the inner logic of the persons in their specific circumstances. The

25

basis for the Laboratory Theatre's *Akropolis* was the situation of Jews in Auschwitz, and particularly those who were kept alive in the camp some time before being exterminated. The actors looked to understand that ununderstandable situation; possibly, they supposed, in extreme oppression there comes an inner way of speaking, a repeated formula – for example, something like, "Still the same?" Each actor discovered his facial mask by repeating a specific inner formula and allowing it to sculpture his face, almost giving the wrinkles.

In essence, they followed the exact process as it occurs in life, where a person's face after he reaches a certain age, begins to take on the characteristics of a mask, because repeated reactions have sculpted the wrinkles. The way in which Grotowski's actors approached facial mask was, therefore, directly linked to the inner logic of the person. In other words, to what Stanislavski called the inner monologue.

But, when I misinterpreted Grotowski's work with facial mask, I just began to fix "masks" with my face muscles. I played many different characters, so for each character I would contort my face into another form that I thought would somehow be intense or interesting. I even constructed these "masks" with a mirror. We began to fix the *exterior forms*, and the inner life of our many improvisations slowly died: we did not have a technique to set this inner life. How could we recapture it, repetition after repetition? The closer we came to performance, the more mechanically the text was spoken. The old poetry, once alive, became more and more empty. I concentrated on my physical movements, facial masks, vocal intonations, and completely lost contact with my partners. By the opening, I had transformed myself into a blind and deaf puppet on stage.

The performance was strongly criticized. It does not surprise me. We had fought to do something more profound than normal theatre; we thought we were superior, but in result we had just created banal theatre. Our actions had become wooden and forced. The key to this disaster lay not in any lack of commitment and, though young, the director was a very intelligent and gifted artist. But despite his and our overflowing commitment, finally we lacked the technique to fix a living process, and the ability to repeat it.

After that experience I acted in two more plays, both performed in Greenwich Village in New York. In these productions,

26

the rehearsal periods being short – three to four weeks – the problems were different. The actors worked not for the play in which they were acting, but for the *next* one: the value of the present work lay only in its function as stepping stone. Each ten-minute break, the actors would run to the telephones to contact their agents to see if they had any jobs or auditions. Everyone was focused on his "career," not on the work at hand. Concentration was completely dispersed; everyone worked for himself.

In these performances, however, the text was spoken a little less mechanically than in the classical tragedy, on which I had worked for nine months. But why? Not because of some technique or true elaboration, but simply because we had less time – there was hardly enough time to memorize the lines, let alone time enough for them to become mechanical! Nevertheless, I must admit, my lines did become lifeless anyway, despite our short rehearsal period; my monologues, in the beginning so full, had, a few weeks later, been reduced to a lifeless echo. I reproduced tones and inflections, not living action.

I realized I had no technique and thought maybe I should go to drama school. Some of the other cast members, who had been more successful than I, had been to drama school; yet something in me was very uneasy about that prospect. I saw that drama schools taught their students a technique to help them succeed in the theatre "business" as it exists, but I was having profound doubts about being in the "business" at all. Did I really want to work in performances in which your acting partner might not be supporting you, but actually playing to make you look bad, because he wanted to make himself look good for a fancy agent sitting in the audience that night? His "super objective" was in the audience. And this was something Stanislavski fought against his entire life.

I no longer knew *for what* I was working. What would I be serving with such work?

These thoughts were troubling me, and one day everything came to a head. I had an appointment with a big theatrical agency; they had seen my work and were ready to discuss "handling" me as an actor. I arrived at the meeting and the agent began by asking me my feelings about art, and what I wanted to achieve in theatre. As I was giving him my reply, he suddenly said to me: "Bob? . . . Yes, get him into that audition at Universal." But my name is

Thomas. . . . I did not know what was going on, so I kept on speaking about art, until I realized that while I had been speaking, his telephone earplug – always stuck in his ear – had suddenly turned on, connecting him to Hollywood: without breaking our conversation and still looking me in the eyes, he had begun making a deal over some other actor in Hollywood.

So I started to think, What does art have to do with this? Was not this talk about art just a lie, to keep my conscience quiet and pumped full of its pseudo-artistic dream, while he and I, together, tried to figure out into what cozy box I might fit, so that I could be best sold as a commodity?

After this meeting I had profound doubts about becoming an actor at all. The only place I had intuited a deep respect for the actor's craft was with Grotowski. If I was going to be an actor, I clearly needed to work with someone who could teach me how to fix the alive process so that it could be repeatable; someone whose artistic ethics had not been corrupted by a "business" demanding the need for an immediately saleable product. Only in the work with Grotowski had I felt such integrity. So I resolved to work with him, no matter what the cost.

I found out that Grotowski would hold a two-month workshop in Italy that summer, and, in the spring, a conference at Hunter College in New York. I decided to attend the conference, in order to ask him in person if I could take part in his summer workshop in Italy.

GROTOWSKI SPEAKS AT HUNTER COLLEGE

I first heard Grotowski speak about physical actions in his 1985 conference at Hunter College in New York City. He gave a lecture on Stanislavski. Among other things, Grotowski spoke about the performance of one Russian actor he had seen in a Tolstoy drama, *The Fruits of Enlightenment*. The character the actor portrayed talks for practically a whole act. He is a professor interested in parapsychological phenomena, who visits the house of some friends and tries to convince those present of his theories. The whole act revolves around this professor's discourse to the other characters. Grotowski said the probability of this performance being boring was high, and the actor's task truly difficult: he had to dominate an immense monologue which, even worse, was a lecture. The performance, however, was on a high level. Why? Thanks to the use the actor made of the "method of physical actions."

Grotowski said that the only props the actor had used, were, for example, the small everyday objects of the professor. As Grotowski spoke, he made use of the objects on the table in front of him: pipe, pipe cleaner, tobacco, etc., in some moments remembering with his own body the performance of this actor, recreating his actions before us.

Yes, he continued, that actor lectured the other characters, but what was his "physical score"? It was *the fight for attention*, the *recognition of allies and adversaries* (through *observing* the listeners), looking for support from the allies, directing his attacks toward characters he suspected as adversaries, etc. This was a *score of battle*, not of conference. Grotowski tried to remember: Perhaps he utilized his small objects? The taking of the cigarette, the lighting of it . . . ? His ballet with the small objects could all have been empty activities, Grotowski said. But it was the *how* and the *why* that made them, not activities, but *physical actions*. Suppose, for instance, the character takes a cigarette; in reality he is stalling, taking time to think of his next argument. He now drinks the water on the table; actually he does so in order to survey the others, to see who is on his side, who agrees with him. Maybe he asks himself, "Have I convinced them or not? Yes, most of them are convinced, but not this fellow in the big chair!" So he resumes his speaking in order to "break" this one, focusing onto him all of his attack.

Grotowski himself took on the small physical actions of the character, and we became his partners, listening: he used the activities with his personal objects (pipe, glass of water, etc.) and turned them into physical actions directed toward us, seeing in us who was on his side and who not. Who was his enemy? An active battle to convince us came to life.

The Russian actor of whom Grotowski spoke had, with his score of physical actions in relation to his partners, transformed a lengthy monologue into a battle. Some years later, I found out that the actor performing the professor of whom Grotowski had spoken was Vasily Toporkov, the disciple of Stanislavski who writes in depth about the "method of physical actions" in his book *Stanislavski in Rehearsal*.[10] Grotowski considers this book to be the most important document – or description – of Stanislavski's way of working on the "method of physical actions."

In his Hunter College lecture, Grotowski also demonstrated another physical action which was at the same time simple and very complex. "For example, let's take the action of 'remember-ing'," he said. "If someone is remembering something, observe what happens to his body." Grotowski tried to remember some-thing: the position of his spine changed, becoming more erect; his head tilted a little down; his hand hung suspended in the air. He said he sensed physically that this memory lay some-where behind him; in this moment it was for him in some precise place a few feet behind his head. This seemed very important: the memory was *precisely located in the space*; and almost imper-ceptibly, but clearly, his body arched toward this place. He enacted all of these physical details with the intent of recalling some forgotten fact, and we saw someone on the verge of remembering something.

In this demonstration, what was the physical action? Grotowski's way of looking for the memory, *and because of that*, his way of keeping the spine, the rhythm of his hand left hanging in the air, the steadiness and the duration of his gaze; it was his internal search for the exact memory which was projected into the space, his body sensing this memory behind him, and subtly reaching back for it. We could clearly read what he was doing, through the physical actions of his body which searched, as if asking, "Where is it? Where is it?"

"Activities are not physical actions," Grotowski repeated many times. He then demonstrated very clearly the difference between physical activities and physical actions. He did so with his glass of water: he lifted the glass to his mouth and drank. An activity, banal and uninteresting, he said. Then he drank the water observing us, stalling his speech to give himself time to think, and size up his opponent. The activity had been turned into a physical action, alive. It now had a specific rhythm, born from what he was doing, in turn born from his circumstances. If I read his body I understood his intention: "Did he have us, his opponents, where he wanted, or not?" He drinks to give himself time to see, judge, make a precise strategy, and then, he begins his attack.

Grotowski always stresses that the work on physical actions is the key to the actor's craft. An actor must be able to repeat the same score many times, and it must be alive and precise each time. How can we do this? What can an actor fix, make secure? His line of physical actions. This becomes like the score for a musician. The line of physical actions must be elaborated in detail and completely memorized. The actor should have absorbed this score to such an extent that he has no need at all to think *what to do next*.

After Grotowski finished speaking, I went up to him. Our conversation was brief. I reminded him that I had worked with him for two weeks at Irvine the previous summer, and asked if I could participate in his workshop that coming summer in Italy. He thought for some seconds and said, "Yes. You and M. can come. No one else." (M. was another actor from Yale who had worked with Grotowski for those two weeks at U. C. Irvine. I later found out that M. had contacted Grotowski by letter to see if he could work with him again that summer.)

During this lecture at Hunter College, I heard for the first time

31

a theoretical explanation of Stanislavski's "method of physical actions." At the time I thought: "I understand. It seems simple enough as a method, logical. Okay, enough of the easy stuff, now how to get to the inner revelation." That summer in Italy, however, I would begin to learn that to understand something with one's mind alone, is a far cry from being able *to do* something. To know something is a different matter, related more to one's ability to do, to put into practice. After this lecture, I naïvely assumed my mental understanding of the "method of physical actions" was sufficient.

THE WORK AT
BOTINACCIO: AN ATTACK
ON DILETTANTISM

Right before I left for Italy that summer, I remember my father
teasing me about my upcoming journey to Europe. Recently I
had given up the saxophone, an instrument I studied seriously
for seven years, and began practicing the Japanese shakuhachi
flute. As I packed my bamboo flute into my knapsack, my father
said, "So, you're off to play to the mountains, eh?" At the time
his comment seemed like a normal father–son jibe. Only later
would I be able to see the truth that lay behind his teasing: the
danger he sensed was that I might become a dilettante, someone
who drifts from here to there without confronting the need for
craft, one who meets life without responsibility. Then however,
I thought nothing of my father's joke. I felt he was just steeped
in the superficialities of normal life, so I went on my way without worrying more about it. I did not expect that dilettantism and
"touristic" behavior were those exact characteristics for which
Grotowski, himself, would severely attack me during the work
that summer in Botinaccio.

Grotowski held his workshop in an old villa on a hilltop in
a Tuscan forest. This brief but dense period of work proved to
be a needed, fatal blow to my ego. The question at hand: dilettantism vs. mastery.

The work session centered on the creation of "mystery plays,"
short individual pieces with a repeatable structure, like mini,
one-man performances. The appearance of a very old song held
great importance in the "mystery play," a song which you
remembered from your youth, for example, one sung by your
mother. First, you had to remember the song: not "Happy
Birthday to You," not "Kumbaya," not a song from the radio,
but an ancient song; it should have roots. It was as if Grotowski

were trying to get us to rediscover any personal connections to tradition we might already have through the songs that had been sung to us as children.

First we saw the "mystery plays" of Grotowski's assistants: the one of Du Yee Chang left in me an especially strong impression. I felt something of his soul had been bared in this action. It was quite intense, and I admired him greatly for the way his body and voice had become one. Though I understood nothing of his "mystery play," the song being in Korean, his native language, I received something and believed him completely.

I planned to arrive at such a level of intensity myself. To accomplish this, I thought I should base my "mystery play" on a very important memory from my early life. I remembered a song which my mother had sung to me as a child, an American slave song. This was the closest I could come to a traditional song. Then I set about making the first draft of my "mystery play." For my presentation I chose a place outside the villa, a clearing in the forest, hoping it would give good atmosphere.

To construct the "mystery play," I remembered a game from my childhood in which my father would dance with me standing on his feet. I made a ritualistic-like stick with leaves attached to it. In my imagination this stick represented my father. I would hold the stick and dance with it as my father, pretending that I was dancing on his toes. This I did while singing the song a few times. Then I would stand the stick upright in a pile of rocks, which represented to me the burial of my father. My father was not actually dead, but this symbolic burial represented the separation of father and son. I thought this deep theme would be highlighted by my intense performance. So my structure was complete, and for the rest I would pour my soul into it through the song.

When it came time to show my first draft, I grew terribly nervous. I don't know if I screamed the song, but everything I did was a blur; I did not see or hear anything. After I finished, since I felt drained, I thought I must have achieved something pretty intense. Then came from Grotowski the fatal words that would become the catchphrase for that summer's work session: "Please repeat." The test against dilettantism.

My goodness, how could I repeat that now? Did he not see I had just bared my soul? I could not possibly have the strength to do it again, I was obviously very tired. How could I muster

34

up all the force needed to do the "mystery play" again with its original intensity? Well, I tried and felt much worse. I eliminated one round of the song to save strength, and did my best to match my original intensity. I knew that the impression I made on Grotowski would be based on my ability to do again the exact actions I had done the first time. So as my body huffed and puffed to recreate my original physical intensity, my mind quickly tried to remember what I had done the first time: my structure had not been so precise, and the first time through, in my enthusiasm, I had added some new elements which I had not practiced before in rehearsals. Now, as I repeated a second time, I tried frantically to remember these new improvised elements, in order to cover up the fact that they had been improvised.

I finished exhausted. My colleague, M., from Yale, was next, and when I saw his work I felt very pleased. What I saw him do was just silly with no sense, I did not perceive any story or revelation in his work. True, his "mystery play" was simple and in moments believable, but inwardly I smiled, patting myself on the back for how profound I had been in my "mystery play," compared to my colleague.

The time for Grotowski's analysis arrived. I was stunned as Grotowski mercilessly attacked my work. I now realize that I had misunderstood three major points.

First: what *I* understood as the story of the "mystery play" and what the others who were watching understood, might be two different things. I naïvely assumed they would understand the same thing as I, that the stick was my father, for example. I thought they would see the story of a boy's traumatic separation from his father, a complex story, rich in meaning to me. But it did not reach them at all. They just saw me sing a song in a forced way, pump an emotional experience, execute an unarticulated dance with a stick, and then stand the stick in a pile of rocks. This could only give them the association of a bad mumbo-jumbo priest. The complex story about the separation of father and son never reached them. The first lesson I grasped from Grotowski's criticism was that the story arriving to those who watch is not necessarily the same as what the actor perceives in his imagination. And as actor as well as director in this situation, it was my responsibility to create *consciously* the story that they would receive.

35

Second: I was using "symbols" in a mistaken way. Rather than doing concrete actions, I represented them symbolically, assuming that those who watched would understand the symbol in the same way I did. For instance, the stick as my father: they had no way of understanding it. I substituted symbols for actions. Instead of reacting to my father before me with a line of actions, remembering truthfully what I had done when I danced on his feet, refinding our precise physical behavior and details of contact between us, I symbolically represented him with a stick, and tried to pump myself emotionally to convey an idea: the traumatic separation of father and son. I had constructed my "mystery play" with symbols that were not understandable, and then pumped "epic emotion" related to some past event.

Third: I thought that the audience would experience the same so-called intensity that I felt while performing, that they too would experience this "epic emotion." I did not see that often I would convince myself of having "felt something," while in reality all I had felt was excited nerves due to the fact that I was "acting" in front of someone. In other words I had mistaken agitated nerves for true emotions; I had avoided true practical work, and tried to pump an emotional state. In his conference in Liège (1986), Grotowski said:

> "Normally, when an actor thinks of intentions, he thinks it is a question of pumping an emotional state in himself. It is not this. The emotional state is very important, but it does not depend on the will. I don't want to be sad: I am sad. I want to love this person: I hate this person, because the emotions are independent of the will. So, everyone who looks to condition actions through emotional states makes a confusion."[11]

Grotowski would often ask us two questions when analyzing the work of someone. First: What did you understand? The persons who had watched would then say what they had understood. Afterwards, the person who had done the "mystery play" was asked to recount the actual story he was trying to tell. In this way we could see how successful the actor had actually been in telling his story. Second: Did you believe? Sometimes a "mystery play" might work when, despite the fact that we did not understand, we believed what the actor had done, and as a result we felt or received something from his work. Then one might say: "I did not understand, but I believed," and the "mystery play" could be said to be on the right track.

In the analysis of the first draft of my "mystery play," not only Grotowski attacked me, but also all the other persons in the workshop. It turned out they neither believed nor understood. I was completely shocked, I thought I had really revealed something. I did not see I was actually trying to jump to the stars with no stairs. I was very spoiled and convinced of my talent. I did not at the time accept the difficult work and sacrifice needed to arrive at true results; I thought that excellence should come by itself.

I was even doubly shocked when all, including Grotowski, praised the work of my friend, M. In my perception, M. had not revealed anything profound. They all claimed, however, they had believed him. This seemed to be the criterion for him to have some material *on which he might begin work.* M.'s "mystery play" had been simple and believable, a possible base on which he could begin the work of construction. This I could not yet understand: "Construction?"

Grotowski sent me back to the drawing board to make my "mystery play" more clear. I should define the situation: What am I trying to do? Was there some invisible partner with me? Where was this partner in the space? What exactly did I do with him? All simple and practical questions. Grotowski insisted that I resolve these small essential problems, but I was still not satisfied. I thought my "mystery play" had not worked – not because of lack of details, truthful details – but because I had not yet found the deep profound story, the right memory to reveal.

After the analysis, at first I tried to follow Grotowski's advice, to work in a precise and detailed way as he had told me. I did not like it very much, I felt it stifled my creativity. So, deciding the story itself must be to blame, I searched my memory and came up with what I thought to be a truer moment from my life. I changed the subject of my "mystery play." Here I broke a rule that was always used in my future work with Grotowski: when structuring a piece, you only have the right to throw something out if you have already *concretely* found something better.

The new subject I tried to portray in my "mystery play" was a childhood memory of being in my crib. I wanted my mother to take me out of the crib. I decided I would kneel on the floor, assuming that this kneeling would indicate my situation to those who were watching. I did not think it necessary to refind my exact physical behavior: in any case, if I knelt, they should be able to understand that I was in a crib and that I was young. I then worked on all the painful details. I tried to figure out from where my mother entered the room, I defined the space choosing a place for the door. Then, why did she enter the room? I tried to answer precise questions. She comes in. I follow her around the room with my look, trying to catch her attention. She comes close. I have an impulse toward her asking her to pick me up. With this impulse I started my slave song. In the middle of the song I have already convinced her to pick me up, so I start rising off my knees. From this "rising off my knees," I assumed those who watched would understand I was being picked up by my mother. I did not think the story could be any clearer.

For some days I worked on this structure, but then I became fed up, impatient. All this work on detail seemed silly: evidently the subject matter was of no value. When I had improvised this line of actions, in the beginning I had experienced all sorts of genuine feelings, but now that I repeated it, it had become dry and dead. I was convinced this new subject still must not be the right one, not being powerful enough to hold my interest.

I felt so bored working on those details. . . . Every time I began to rehearse I became very sleepy, a wave of tiredness came over me. I became depressed. "This boredom," I thought, "must come from the fact that my story is not interesting." I did not realize I was merely succumbing to the first downward wave that was pushing me off course, keeping me from accomplishing my task.

I also convinced myself that the problem lay in the song. How was I to be expected to have a traditional song? My family was not religious, and we were American at that. I had no tradition, of course I did not know any good old songs! How could I create a meaningful "mystery play" without a true song? I was jealous of the European participants who knew many beautiful songs: if they sung these songs simply, often something magical happened.

With this logic I decided the only way to proceed was to compose my own song. I would just have to be responsible for creating my own "traditional song." I remembered the first melody I ever composed on the piano as a child, and using it as a base I created a song, weaving into it the melodic way my mother used to call my name from afar. In this way I composed my song so that it connected my early life.

My "mystery play" this time lasted about fifteen minutes, though we had been clearly asked they be no longer than two or three. I started off huddled in the corner singing. I then exploded out into the center of the space and did an intense dance for a long time. At one point I did a softer dance in an open shirt, remembering with my body how my mother used to dance around our house in only a long shirt calling out softly, "I am a naked bird, I am a naked bird."

When it came time to present this "mystery play" to Grotowski and the others, I was electrified. I thought my song would certainly solve the problem and be a revelation to all; they probably would not even be able to tell that it was not a true traditional song. What more just approach could there be for me, being an American, a child without tradition?

I did my "mystery play." A big silence followed as I went to sit down. In that silence I judged my success. Then came a strange noise, my friend M. was crying. It started softly and gradually turned into sobs. He was truly in tears. He even collapsed over, putting his head down in the lap of the girl next to him. He was really crying. I thought, "My goodness, my 'mystery play' must have been really good. M. is even crying." I was in heaven: someone watching had had a true cathartic experience.

Then M. suddenly stopped crying and stood up. His crying had been the surprise beginning to his new "mystery play"; it did not have anything to do with my work at all, it had been part of his own. I was crushed. I had been completely mistaken. I frantically looked around at the other faces to see if I could judge in their eyes my success, but they were already intent on watching M.'s work.

We went downstairs to the kitchen on break, and by that time I had once again convinced myself of my triumph. As I prepared my snack, I glowed with self-satisfaction. Then, here comes Grotowski. He's walking in my direction, smiling, and, "Oh, I must have been good," I think. "He is coming to . . . me? Yes! Here he comes." And with a big smile he said: "That was awful! That was just incredibly awful! I don't think I have ever seen anything so bad," and walked away. As he spoke he had been smiling all the time, almost on the verge of laughter.

I was devastated. My ego had never received such a blow. I could not understand. I became completely depressed.

In his analysis later, Grotowski said the songs must *not be improvised*. I think I was accused of being altogether false in my "mystery play," nothing was believable or understandable. He said in what I had done there was no value, except for two small moments: the first was in the corner, when I started to sing very softly, but as soon as I became loud it had lost all value; the second was when I was in the open shirt remembering with my body my mother's way of dancing. He said if he were working on this "mystery play," he would throw away everything except these two small moments, and explore them to see what they held.

He attacked me for being a "tourist." In the terminology of Grotowski, a "tourist" is someone who travels around with no roots, a person who goes from place to place superficially. An artist can also work "touristically": being addicted to the thrill of first improvisation, he has no patience to work on structure. He becomes bored when his nerves are not agitated, and discards everything to find a new proposition that will excite his nerves again. Such an artist passes from first draft to first draft without ever delving deep, without exploring one territory fully. True art, Grotowski said, is like a plumb line which does not move side to side. In the beginning of work on a "mystery play," the difficulty is to find the right song, and then the right story to go with the song. But once these have been found, it will take many many drafts and hard, patient work to arrive at a structure of any quality. Grotowski stressed that the process is not easy, and the fruits appear only, and maybe, at the end of a long road. By not developing the first draft of my "mystery play," I had worked "touristically." I had not made more clear my first proposition. I became restless when confronted with technical work, and, since I no longer found it immediately gratifying, I switched topic even improvising a song to have the feeling of "new," justifying my "tourism" by a claimed lack of tradition. Grotowski indicated the two fragments on which he thought I must concentrate, and sent me back to work.

Accustomed to immediate success in my life, I could not understand my present difficulty. Normally I didn't have to work so much; creating used to come naturally, without great effort. But now the work seemed immense and heavy. I started to become paranoid, thinking Grotowski really didn't like me.

At this point, I would like to step aside from the flow of my memories to make an observation about Grotowski's criticisms. When I began to work with Grotowski, I thought his assistants were untouchable, that they could do no wrong. This was not the case at all. In reality, he expected more of his assistants than of us, as participants. He created more of a challenging situation for them. The closer you worked with Grotowski, the more he expected; the more you should fight to maintain any level you had already attained, and go forward toward new discoveries. Many times he would ruthlessly criticize the work of his assistants if they had led a fragment of work mechanically, replacing true process with empty form. He tested everyone around him, requesting of them their personal highest level. Grotowski was not just attacking me, he attacked everywhere he perceived descent in quality. But at the time, I took all of his attacks personally. I thought he must severely dislike me.

I went back to my "mystery play" and again managed to convince myself that I had not yet found the right subject. I once again changed topic. This time I chose the topic of my blind grandmother. I based my new "mystery play" on her going to the church to pray for the doctor who had blinded her by giving her the wrong medication. When I started to explore with my own body the physicality of my grandmother, I began to feel her presence, and was carried away by the feeling the "tourist" loves so much: the thrill of the first improvisation. Well, by that time I had already heard Grotowski enough to know I should work on precise details, so I set out to construct the church in the workspace, to know the placement of all of the imaginary objects. I then remembered her body with mine, how she walked and how, being blind, she would feel her way toward the altar. But a voice started to speak inside me, saying I was just once again being a "tourist," going to the side. Most of the other persons in the workshop were already on their third elaboration of one "mystery play" and I was still exploring first drafts. I saw from their work that what Grotowski had said about construction was true. In the beginning many "mystery plays" seemed simple and boring, but by the third or fourth elaborations I already noticed in them a startling and unexpected quality: the compositions had become more interesting as the actors worked in depth on one subject. I began to dread the next demonstration, anticipating exposure as a full-fledged "tourist" with neither patience nor technique, someone who wanders around in a bum-like way without purpose, continually avoiding any true responsibility.

I was becoming more and more depressed. My friend M., noticing my state, even gave me special vitamins, hoping they would give me some force. Then one day in the kitchen Grotowski came in and gave me a pastry, for what seemed to be no reason. I became so happy. Just the fact that he had given me a little piece of cake which he brought all the way from Florence made me so very happy. It was an entirely unexpected present. "He doesn't hate me after all," I thought.

Well, in his next analysis I learned *why* he gave me the cake. He said I was in a very difficult situation. I had been going through life passing from explosion to explosion, and if I continued to live in this way I would soon have no more inner fire left, only ashes. He said, now you still have a little fire, a very small one but it is almost completely extinguished. Your chances of succeeding in the commercial theatre are very slim. You will not fit into any category easily, and also your facial features, with the upper lip thinner than the lower lip, give the impression that when your face is relaxed you are pouting. He said, for this reason you will probably not be hired for the movies, though no one will ever say this is the reason, or even see so themselves. The way for you will be very difficult, and there is almost no hope.

My only chance, he said, was if I made an incredibly long work, which would be like entering a dark tunnel in which I would not know if there would ever be light at the end. Then and only then would I have the chance to discover something. And this discovery would depend upon the fact that I should start, now, working as if I was an old peasant, like an old peasant in the time before machines. I should do all my little tasks honestly without being in a hurry, one after another. When we see an old peasant working, Grotowski said, we can think he is slow. A younger person works next to him, and we think this young one, with his rhythm fast and staccato, will accomplish the job quicker. The young person hurries, but at the end of the day we see that the old peasant has accomplished more, working slowly, continuously, one task after the next. Because of his continuity he wastes nothing. Through experience the old peasant knows that to work continually with a steady rhythm burns less energy than to stop and start, stop and start. I should find this rhythm of work in which every movement economizes and nothing is wasted. He said he gave me the cake the other day to see my facial reaction. My face had lost its expressiveness, he said. Either it was blank or with a big smile, there were no in-betweens, no shades or colors. I should fight this problem by holding back the extreme reactions to find again my different natural expressions.

After he had told me all this I was completely devastated. He spoke with such authority. I think I went upstairs to cry. It was as if a death sentence had been pronounced. I sensed the truth in everything he said. My ego was crushed, my illusions shattered.

Shortly after that analysis, one of the assistants told me he personally thought I should come to work with Grotowski in Irvine for one year; and if I wanted, he would propose me to Grotowski as a candidate. This greatly surprised me. I said I clearly was not doing well in the work that summer, and asked what made him think I should go to Irvine. He said, Grotowski is only hard on you because he sees something in you; if he did not see in you some possibility, he would not be so hard. I said I was not sure I was right for the work. He replied I could only know really if I was right for the work, if I did it for one year; only then would I be able to see if I was receiving something, whether I was right for the work and the work right for me.

The workshop that summer was scheduled for two months, but my ego was so crushed I could not stay. I left after the first month. I did not show the last version of the "mystery play" about my grandmother. I knew I had just been a "tourist," again going to the side for the immediate excitation of improvisation. I could not face being exposed for a third time as a "tourist."

Right before I left Italy, I went to Grotowski's public conference in Florence (1985), where he strongly attacked tourism and dilettantism in artists. I knew he was referring directly to the problems he had found in me, as well as others he was working with that summer in Botinaccio:

"In this field one of the tests is a kind of individual ethnodrama, in which the starting point is an old song

43

linked to the ethnic-religious tradition of the person in question. One begins to work with this song as if, in it, was codified in potentiality (movement, action, rhythm. . .) a totality. It's like an ethnodrama in the collective traditional sense, but here, it is *one* person who acts with *one* song and *alone*. So, immediately with modern people, there appears the following problem: you find something, a small structure around the song, then, parallelly, you construct a new version, and parallel to that a third. This means that you always stay at the first level – superficial, let's say, as if the all fresh proposal excited the nerves and gave us the illusion of something. This means that you are working going sideways – and not like someone digging a well. That's the difference between the dilettante and the non-dilettante. The dilettante may make something beautiful, more or less superficially, through this excitation of the nerves in the first improvisation. But it is to sculpt in smoke. It always disappears. The dilettante searches 'sideways.'[. . .] This has nothing to do with the construction of cathedrals, that always have a keystone. It is exactly the plumb line that determines the value. But with an individual ethnodrama, it is a difficult thing to achieve, because you pass through crises. The first proposal: it works. After, you have to eliminate that which isn't necessary and reconstruct it in a more compact manner. You go through periods of work that are 'lifeless.' It's a kind of crisis, of boredom. Many technical problems have to be solved: for example the montage, like in film. You must rebuild, and rememorize the first proposition (the line of small physical actions), but eliminating all the actions that are not absolutely necessary. You must, therefore, make cuts, and then know how to join the different fragments. For instance, you can apply the following principle: line of the physical actions – stop – elimination of a fragment – stop – line of the physical actions. Like in cinema, the sequence in movement stops on a fixed image – we cut – another fixed image marks the beginning of a new sequence in movement. This gives: physical action – stop – stop – physical action. But what must be done with the cut, with the hole? At the first stop you are, let's say, standing with the arms up and, at the second stop, sitting with the arms down. One of the solutions consists then in carrying out the passage from one position to the other as a technical demonstration of ability, almost a ballet, a game of ability. It is only one possibility among others. But in any case this requires much time to be done. You must also resolve this other problem: the stop should not be mechanical, but like a frozen waterfall: I mean that all the drive of the movement is there, but stopped. The same thing for that which concerns the stop starting the next fragment of action: still motionless, it must be already in the body, otherwise it does not work. Then you have the problem of the adjustment between the 'audio' and the 'visual.' If at the moment of the cut you have a song, should the song be cut or not? You must decide: What is the river and what is the boat? If the river is the song and the physical actions the boat, then evidently the river must not be interrupted – so the song should not be broken but modulate the physical actions. But most often it is the contrary which is valid: the physical actions are the river and modulate the way of singing. You must know what you choose. And all this example about the montage concerns only the elimination of a fragment; but there is also the problem of insertions, when you take a fragment from another place in your proposition in order to insert it between two stops.

As I said before, this type of work passes through moments of crisis. You arrive at elements more and more compact. Then, your body must completely absorb all this and recover its organic reactions. You must turn back, toward *the seed* of the first proposition and find that which, from the point of view of this primary motivation, requires a new restructuring of the whole. So the work does not develop 'to the side, to the side' but as with the plumb line and always through phases of organicity, of crisis, of organicity, etc. We can say that each phase of spontaneity of life is always followed by a phase of technical absorption.

You must face all of the classical questions of the performing arts. For example: But who is the person who sings the song? Is it you? But if it is a song from your grandmother, is it still you? But if you are discovering in you your grandmother, through your body's impulses, then it's neither 'you' nor 'your grandmother who had sung': it's you exploring your grandmother who sings. Yet it can be that you go further back, toward some place, toward some time difficult to imagine, when for the first time someone sang this song. I'm speaking about a true traditional song, which is anonymous. We say: It's the people who sang. But among these people, there was someone who began. You have the song, you must ask yourself where this song began.

Perhaps it was the moment of tending a fire in the mountains on which someone was looking after animals. And to keep warm in front of this fire someone began to repeat the opening words. It wasn't a song yet, it was an incantation. A primary incantation that someone repeated. You look at the song and ask yourself: Where is this primary incantation? In which words? Maybe these words have already disappeared? Maybe the person in question had sung other words, or a phrase other than the one you sing, and maybe another person developed this first nucleus. But if you are capable of going with this song towards the beginning, it is not any longer your grandmother who sings, but someone from your lineage, from your country, from your village, from the place where the village was, the village of your parents, of your grandparents. In the way of singing itself the space is codified. One sings differently in the mountains and in the plains. In the mountains one sings from one high place to another, so the voice is thrown like an arc. You gradually refind the first incantations. You refind the landscape, the fire, the animals, maybe you began to sing because you had a fear of the solitude. Did you look for others? Did it happen in the mountains? If you were on a mountain, the others were on another mountain. Who was this person who sang thus? Was this person young or old? Finally you will discover that you come from somewhere. As one says in a French expression, 'Tu es le fils de quelqu'un' (You are someone's son). You are not a vagabond, you come from somewhere, from some country, from someplace, from some landscape. There were real people around you, near or far. It's you two hundred, three hundred, four hundred, or one thousand years ago, but it's you. Because he who began to sing the first words was someone's son, from somewhere, from someplace, so, if you refind this, you are someone's son. If you do not refind it, you are not someone's son; you are cut off, sterile, barren."[12]

I left Grotowski's workshop with the excuse that my friend and I wanted to see Peter Brook's *Mahabharata* in Avignon. We did not even have tickets. Even my leaving was tourism; I left hoping to find a more comfortable place to work, one which would tolerate my addiction to so-called spontaneity.

I participated in a few workshops of Rena Mirecka, a remarkable actress of the Laboratory Theatre; there my "tourism" did not create problems. I was attracted to this work with Rena on improvisations. It was very life-giving. But after these workshops, I started to feel that if the work with Grotowski had been a paternal nightmare, then maybe there was the danger that work with Rena might become for me a maternal daydream. I began to think, for my development in the long run, maybe the paternal nightmare would be more useful to undergo. I saw the need to commit myself to something, but I was still not convinced the work with Grotowski was the right thing. I traveled to Denmark where I observed the work of the Odin Theatre, and was struck by the composition of their performances and the precision of their actors. This impressed me greatly and I asked myself if I had not found my place. Then – in the Odin – I saw for the first time all the films of Grotowski's old theatre performances. I was completely blown away. They were so profound and true. In the films of Grotowski's work I witnessed such amazing depth of individual expression, and this stream of life was all miraculously working in a very definite structure. Grotowski somehow worked where exactness and human life converged on an inexplicably high level. He must have arrived at that level with his actors, demanding of them the same rigor he had demanded of us at Botinaccio, and more.

At that moment I decided to see whether Grotowski would accept me to work with him in California for one year, as his assistant had suggested. My ego, however, was still hesitant. I had to reason with it, saying I actually had no personal discipline, and if I wanted to accomplish anything in my life I

47

would need personal discipline. Even if I learned nothing else from Grotowski, I would surely learn that.

I called Grotowski's assistant, and the reply came back from Grotowski that I could come to work with them in California on the condition that I agreed to stay for one year. I agreed.

ONE YEAR
WITH GROTOWSKI IN
OBJECTIVE DRAMA

I left to work with Grotowski without really understanding my
reasons for going. Faced with my ego, I had difficulty justifying
the trip: Grotowski had been so tough on me in Italy. I guess
different forces were driving me. I needed personal discipline.
Grotowski was right, through laziness and impatience I just
made moves to the side in my work. I always thought, however,
this came from the fact that I had not yet found the right thing to
do. I still think there is some truth in that. I had taken saxophone
very seriously up to a point, and then stopped working. I did not
have the incentive to break through to a level of total domination
of the instrument because something inside me had said, this is
not your place. From that point on, I relied on youthful energy
alone to carry me through jazz sessions in which I improvised.
But that worked less and less. The older I became the more the
demand grew for quality of craftsmanship.

Grotowski touched on this point many times when speaking
about the question of "tourism." When you are young, he said,
people let you get away with not having true technique because
your energy is fresh and charming. Here, Grotowski always
instanced Zeami's expression: the "flower of youth." But woe to
you if you pass out of the "flower of youth" without developing the "flower of craft," the flower of mastery. It's like the story
of the shoemaker, Grotowski said. When the shoemaker is
young, people watch him work and exclaim, "What a beautiful
shoemaker, how full of life!" A few years later, however, they
start to demand, "But . . . these shoes? The quality of the shoes?"

This was clearly my case. In my "flower of youth," I had
some sort of flame and this carried me when my craft was still
undeveloped. When I first worked with Grotowski in California,

right after university, I was still in the "flower of youth," riding on its charm. One year later in Italy, however, Grotowski began demanding to see the quality of my "shoes," but there was none. I had not developed any capacity.

I now know that in Botinaccio that summer, Grotowski was asking himself: "In this year away from me has Thomas gained or lost?" He was seeing that I had almost completely lost the "flower of youth," and had not gained anything on the level of the "flower of craft." Grotowski saw me at a crucial moment in which I would either make or break my artistic life. I am deeply indebted to him for how hard he was on me that summer; his strong criticisms were exactly what I needed. Without that kind of blow, I would have gone on behaving like someone still in the "flower of youth" when that flower had already wilted, and as time passed, I would have had less and less force to build anything; and then, enamored of my past youth, I would have spent my time uselessly trying to recapture it, never reaching mastery in anything. I would have become completely dilettante.

When Grotowski spoke about the "flower of youth," he often stressed that this special time must not be wasted. By its nature it does not last very long, for some people a little longer than for others, but when it fades it vanishes swiftly. From one day to the next that flower could be gone. In the traditional way of development, you should already have in hand the "flower of mastery" by the time the "flower of youth" dies. Therefore, the "flower of youth" should not be wasted by passing from explosion to explosion, as I was doing, but its force and vitality utilized consciously in order to construct the "flower of craft."

In the year I worked in New York as an actor – in that short year – I had started to become old. At the time, this I could not see. When I had first gone to work with Grotowski in California, I had just left the undergraduate university system, and even though this system has a lot to be contested, it structured my life, keeping me active and under some stress, raising my level of energy. The year I spent in New York, I had no such rigorous structure. My body and mind in one crucial year became immersed in a very heavy inertia; there was no structure to keep me alert. The work I did in theatre was not demanding, the schedule never lasted more than eight hours a day, and much of my time I wasted waiting and being passive. Because of this passivity, I had aged drastically: from one year

50

to the next, I had become a different person, of a much lower quality, and did not even know it. Grotowski's shock to me at Botinaccio was like a last signal, a warning sign I could either accept or reject. Much was at stake that summer which would indicate the path of my future life.

Yet something in me was alive enough to realize that I did not have the discipline to break through to a higher level of craft. I was lazy, and the only person I knew who would surely put the needed demands on me to break this laziness, was Grotowski. From the short time I had worked with him, I saw that he asked for total commitment from his colleagues. No limitation was set on our daily schedule – sometimes lasting fifteen hours or more – and often the work was quite physically strenuous.

When it spoke, which was often, my wounded ego did not completely accept the work with Grotowski: it had difficulty tolerating this man who had been so tough on it. But something much deeper in me really wanted my work with Grotowski to succeed. I set out for California.

The Objective Drama Program had no funding to pay us. So, upon arriving in California with almost no money, I found a job as a cashier at a local mall to pay my apartment and expenses. That job I worked about five hours a day; then I would go home for a quick nap before the car from Grotowski's Program would drive by to take me down to Irvine, where we would work into the night, normally from six in the evening until about two in the morning. The schedule was tough and I was almost continually exhausted. This did not discourage me, however. I found it invigorating after the last year I had spent in New York where work was inconsistent. Because of this full schedule, some interesting changes also manifested themselves in my sleeping: whenever I would arrive home, the instant my head hit the pillow I would be fast asleep.

That year, the work with Grotowski centered on what would later come to be called the "Main *Action*." It took one year for this "Main *Action*" to be completed and, while we worked, its gradual formation seemed inexplicable to me; at the time it seemed as if everything molded and modified itself like in a dream. There were nine of us in the "performance team" at the Objective Drama Program. "Performance team" seemed rather a strange term to describe us because, to my knowledge, we were not going to give performances. The name did serve well one purpose, however: it silenced my ego which still really wanted to perform and had difficulty accepting the idea of pure theatre research. The name "performance team" kept it quiet, dreaming that maybe someday there would be a performance.

Besides the other elements of work, the "performance team" started to do a training, mainly a physical and acrobatic training, based on exercises that one of the "team" members had learned in Poland with the Laboratory Theatre. These exercises seemed designed to get our group into general physical condition which lacked in some members, especially myself.

Years later, Grotowski told me that the work involved in the creation of the "Main *Action*" had served as a trap for me. Grotowski was looking for someone who he would try to teach and with whom he would work directly. Still unsure as to who he would concentrate his efforts on, he used this year and this "*Action*" as a trap to find the right candidate. Of course, at the time none of us knew this. Or at least I was not aware of it.

Each day we did Motions, a very demanding exercise coming from the Theatre of Sources (in the last period of the Laboratory Theatre). Then and after, Motions was gradually transformed and re-elaborated. The structure of Motions was filtrated between 1979 and 1987. After 1987 the structuration was finalized, based on minute details. I learned the initial structure of Motions during the two-week workshop I attended at the Objective Drama Program in 1984. Ever since, Motions has remained a stable element of our work.

As our ability to do Motions grew, little by little it had to become more precise. Motions is in part an exercise for the "circulation of attention," so when certain elements after many years became easy for us to execute, a new level of precision had to be added to make the exercise again a challenge. Indeed, the work on Motions was, and still is, in progress. There exist many levels on which it can be executed. I now describe the work on Motions and a few of the possible mistakes involved.

Motions is a series of stretches/positions of the body. Its structure is fairly simple, and on its *first superficial* level can be taught quickly. In a brief work session of four days, for example, a participant might learn this *first superficial* level and leave the session mistakenly thinking he has actually learned Motions.

He might think he now knows how to do something practical and simple, and then assume that the next step is to go and teach Motions. Later, when we were conducting selections in Italy, even if we had informed the candidates about this possible misunderstanding, some went on to give their own workshops "teaching" Motions, when in reality they had only worked with us for one week or less. Among such participants, some taught Motions in theatre schools, and others put the entire structure or fragments of it into theatre performances. In this way, the essence of the exercise is destroyed, and many mistakes are passed on.

Motions is deceiving; on the surface it seems very simple but it is not. To really approach even one of its elements, for example the "primal position," each of us who now practices Motions has invested years of systematic work.

The "primal position" is the starting point of Motions, a position of readiness from which the body can move immediately in any direction. When I first learned Motions at Irvine, I was told that from the "primal position" I should be able to defend myself from attack. An assistant of Grotowski had taken me to the edge of the desert to teach me Motions, and the first thing he showed me was this "primal position." When I saw him take this stance, I thought he looked like a little rocket about to take off, or a fighter plane in mid-flight soaring through the sky.

In his text, "Tu es le fils de quelqu'un," Grotowski speaks of the roots of the "primal position":

"Why do the African hunter of the Kalahari, the French hunter of Saintonge, the Bengali hunter, or the Huichol hunter of Mexico all adopt – while they hunt – a certain position of the body in which the spine is slightly inclined, the knees slightly bent, a position held at the base of the body by the sacrum-pelvis complex? And why can this position lead to only one type of rhythmical movement? And what is the utility of this way of walking? There is a level of analysis which is very simple, very easy: if the weight of the body is on one leg, in the moment of displacing the other leg, you don't make noise, and also you displace in a continuous, slow way. Suddenly the animals cannot spot you.

But this is not the essential. The essential is that there

53

exists a certain primary position of the human body. It's a position so ancient that maybe it was that, not only of homo sapiens, but also of homo erectus, and which concerns in some way the appearance of the human species."[13]

There is no walking in Motions. The "primal position" in Motions involves a certain way of standing at precise moments during the course of the exercise.

With the exception of the "primal position," Motions is a series of stretches. The stretches are simple (one can see some similarities to hatha yoga, but it is different). There are three cycles of stretches/positions. Each cycle is one specific stretch/position executed four times, once toward each of the four cardinal directions; turning from one direction to the next is done standing on the same spot. Separating each cycle is a stretch called nadir/zenith, a quick stretch down followed by a quick one up.

When I learned Motions I was told that, when doing them outside, in the forest for example, I should not disturb the life around. Consequently, turning from one direction to another, I should do so slowly and silently, in a way that would not provoke any change in my surroundings. I noticed that if I made noise while turning, shuffling my feet for example, the song of the bird I was hearing was interrupted; the bird had probably stopped to hear what had happened. In that moment I knew I had disturbed. The turning should be done in such a way that I *did not disturb*, and in order to know if I was disturbing or not I should *hear*.

There is also a specific way of seeing in Motions. We were told not to "grasp" things with our vision: we should not see like sharpshooters with our eyes fixing upon an object, but see as if through a big open window. We should see what is in front of us.

At first I learned Motions superficially; the workshop at Irvine lasted only two weeks. When I went back to New York to act, I naïvely wanted to apply something of Motions in a performance. So I tried to use this type of "open vision" on the stage. The result was of course catastrophic; trying to apply something from Motions out of its context was a big mistake – I saw nothing. This "seeing nothing" can be a problem for those who do Motions for a short period of time. Motions is an exercise which can give results only if practiced almost every day, and

54

in Motions one must continually fight against this "zombie look," the dead eyes that see nothing. You must see what is before you and hear what is around you in each moment of the exercise. *And in the same time be present to your own body*: "see that you are seeing, hear that you are hearing."

After we had practiced Motions for some years, the structure became more easy for us, so we had to make it more exact in order that the exercise could once again be a trap for our attention. We started to concentrate on the synchronization of even smaller details, fighting to arrive at a level in which each of the small movements of the persons doing the exercise would be in total synchronization: each small impulsion, the angles of the bodies, the raising and putting down of the feet, etc.

A common mistake in Motions, which we always have to fight against, is when a stretch becomes replaced by a static position. Grotowski strongly corrects us when we "no longer stretch": each position should be *arrived at because we are stretching*, not because we are "keeping the form," an aesthetic position, with our body.

Besides Motions and the physical training, each day the "performance team" did something called "the River." This was a flow of several different Haitian songs together with a dance and very simple improvised reactions. But the main thrust of our work went toward the creation of the "Main *Action*." To arrive at this, each of us began working on small "individual structures," based on fragments of a text thousands of years old, found in Egypt. The "performance team" members, however, never received from Grotowski any precise data about the origin of that text, or about the translators, etc. Grotowski still repeated: the text speaks by itself.

The work on the "Main *Action*" was organized as follows: one of the assistants, Jim Slowiak, led the group in finding and elaborating a structure. Grotowski himself, often not present in the beginning stages of work, would come in when we had prepared a draft to show him, or had accomplished some task he had given us. Jim, who functioned as Grotowski's assistant director in the Objective Drama Program, conducted the practical day-to-day work with the "performance team." A great burden lay on Jim: he would help us create and prepare the structures and then Grotowski would come in, make comments

55

and corrections. We would then go back to work with Jim in order to make the needed revisions.

This period is reminiscent of the work Stanislavski conducted in the final period of his life, when he concentrated his attention on a small group of actors, not to create a performance, but to perfect the technique of those specific actors while working on Molière's *Tartuffe*. In those rehearsals, Kedrov shouldered much responsibility, working with the other actors on assignments Stanislavski had given them. In fact Stanislavski, because of his failing health, was often not present. When the actors arrived at a certain stage in the rehearsals, Stanislavski would come in and work directly, making all of the needed corrections, pointing them in the right direction, making sure they understood where they had been mistaken. This process is clearly outlined by Toporkov in his book *Stanislavski in Rehearsal*. Our work in the Objective Drama Program was very similar. A great part of the responsibility fell on Jim, who to a certain extent had the task of making the "Main *Action*" appear.

As a "pretext" for creating the structure, we started with the "Watching" (described below). We departed from this initial base which through time would adapt and change, and as new elements appeared and were added, eventually the "Watching" itself was no longer recognizable. It had gradually disappeared as the "Main *Action*" appeared. It was an amazing process of transformation.

The "Watching" was like a very long game of "follow the leader." It had a precise but loose structure of simple sequences, almost physical games, and was led by one person. All of the others had to follow in the tempo of the leader, but each in his own individual stream. The whole event had to be silent, no sounds from the floor and no sounds from breathing.

At that stage of the work the "Watching" had become a very difficult test of endurance, like a warrior's game. It could go on for a very long time, and often afterwards everyone had large blisters on their feet from the movements and quick turns involved. During this first year I was always limping home to pop and disinfect foot blisters. Grotowski always said it was possible to do the "Watching" without getting blisters, but we had to discover the way. At the time, I did not believe him. After one year, however, I did stop getting blisters and now in the work I never do. He was right: the body had found its natural way of stepping.

In the "Watching," my problem was to discover how to move silently. Especially during the sequence with dance, I always made an enormous amount of noise with my feet. Still interested in physical and emotional explosions, I would enter into a very big dance and inevitably stamp my feet. Afterwards, Jim would tell me how much noise I had made and I was shocked: I had not heard any noise at all, I thought I had been totally silent. I realized that, in order not to make noise, I would have to be *attentive*; but my attention was so dispersed that during the entire "Watching," I might only have been truly hearing for some seconds. Right after we began, I would lose concentration and no longer be present in order to hear if I was making noise or not. My rate of attention was remarkably slow. Where did I go in these moments when I made noise and did not hear it? This became the key question for me.

Every day that we did the "Watching," Jim would get angry at me for making noise. So as not to make noise, I would have to awaken my attention and watch ("watching," in effect) all the time. Hence the name. From the "Watching" it was possible to see who was attentive and who not, who had quick attention and reactions, whose body was awake. The body, in fact, had to react to the propositions of the leader with lightning speed.

Jim also often accused me of not seeing in the "Watching." It took me a very long time to be able to see anything, we were moving so fast. Often, though, I would just look down and go into "my own world," which was part of my way of pumping. Whenever I tried to do something deep and intense I would disconnect from my partners and look down to the floor. Then from Jim always came the reaction, "Don't look down!" This question of seeing was also part of the general waking-up process I needed. These games shocked one into being alert. Nevertheless, for a long time, I still lost contact with the others and the leader, drowning in those moments in my own thoughts. For someone who observed, my absence was apparent, but I, being lost, did not even know I was stamping my feet. It was as if I were fast asleep. When I remembered, and succeeded in not making noise and in seeing the others, it was as if I had woken up for a moment out of an inner stupor. Jim constantly fought for me to wake up and watch.

A few months into the work, Grotowski invited us over to his house, and showed us a typed copy of the ancient text (mentioned above), divided into small fragments. One after the other we went into an adjoining room to read the text alone, while the rest of us discussed and analyzed with Grotowski various details from the work. After we had all read the text, each of us selected two small fragments that were for him most meaningful. Grotowski then asked each of us to create a song for each of the two fragments we had chosen, and then with these two songs, to create two "individual structures": something along the line of a "mystery play," but now the song was to be of our creation; the words, those of the two fragments we had chosen from the ancient text.

I became scared. The work we had been doing up to that point was related to improvisation within a structure. I knew, however, that when Grotowski started to speak about "individual structure," he was speaking of something that had to be precise and repeatable, like a mini-performance. And, of course, this would call for craftsmanship and the ability to repeat. I was flooded by fearful images as I remembered how I had failed so miserably in this domain the previous summer in Italy.

In order to compose the songs for these fragments I listened to some old Black American songs, basing my melodies loosely on this way of singing. Then, I began to look for the subject: again I wanted to find something close to me, something emotionally very important. I remembered that the first time I had read the fragments, one of them, which I eventually chose, had upon first reading provoked in me the association of a recurring dream I had had as a child. I decided to base my "individual structure" on this dream.

I arrive at a house in the night. It is dark. I do not go into the house, perhaps it is locked. I turn to the right and walk a few steps in front of the house. There I see on the ground an incredible blackness. I look down. It is a hole. I fall into the hole. My body falls for a long time twisting in the air. To stop the dream, I had an imaginary control box in my hand, which had a red button and a green button. I always took this invisible control box to bed with me. When I pushed the green button I would wake up: I would be falling in the hole until I pushed the green button. Sometimes when I "woke up," I would find myself in my bed, but in reality I was still dreaming; now dreaming that I was in my exact room. I turned to the window, and the devil, very classic-looking, with horns on his head and a red

58

suit, would open the window and climb in from the fire escape. If I pushed the red button I could always make him disappear.

Well, I wanted to represent this dream with my "individual structure." I was determined to be precise. I did not want to make the same mistakes I had made that summer in Italy. But now, because I was afraid of making the structure too long, I exaggerated in the opposite direction, making it too short. I think it lasted only thirty seconds. Again I worked with "symbols." When I constructed the "individual structure," I used "symbols" for the different elements of the dream. Then I decided in which moments I should sing the song. I still did not trust in the doing of actions alone, simple and true. I was still pumping emotionally every symbol to make it seem important. Instead of honestly executing the "structure," I tried to convey my deep emotional participation, which simply blocked whoever was watching from understanding what I was doing. I again forgot the truth that Grotowski called the key to the actor's craft: "emotions are independent of the will."[14]

I was not simply doing actions; rather, I made some sort of interpretation of them since I did not trust that the truth of simple, clear actions would be enough. For example, in the beginning of my "individual structure," I lay down on the floor – this was meant to indicate that I was sleeping. On the floor I started to sing the song, and then I stood up – this was meant to indicate that I stood up into a dream world. I took a few steps which signified my walk to the dark house. I saw the hole. Then came the most dramatic moment which I liked best: I fell into the hole and as I fell, would scream. I did not know how to create this falling physically, so I represented it with a symbol. I let out a loud scream and arched back into the yoga "bridge" position, supporting myself with one hand. I then dropped to the ground, immobile, which signified the return to my bed, asleep.

Because I had again composed my "individual structure" with symbols of actions and not with actions themselves, again the story could not be clear for a person watching. I also left out some of the dream's key elements, forgetting to use them in the "individual structure": for instance, the special box which I had in my hand, and the presence of the devil.

Since I did not construct the logical line of physical actions as they had taken place in the dream, I never gave myself the chance to believe in what I was doing. And since I could not believe in what I was doing, someone watching would never be able to either. I represented actions, I gave signs in their stead. I did not really do them. Rather than remembering with my body exactly how I had reacted while falling through the air – refinding all the exact impulses my body (my dreaming-body) had had during the fall, I represented all this with a form, and into this form tried to pour the emotion I had felt in that moment. I invented a form with my mind, intended to represent something the body had actually experienced. Then I tried to execute that form, and suck forth the emotion that had been present in the dream itself. But the body did not have any logical behavior in which it could believe.

I also did not understand that the body might remember by itself. If I let my body do its own work, let it remember its own way of falling, the body might start to trust in the truthfulness of its process, and itself remember the experience of falling. If this were done truthfully enough, the emotion might follow along, as had happened in the dream, where there was the reality of the dreaming-body's fall, and then the specific reaction of terror, provoked by what the body was experiencing. First came the fall and then the emotion.

After I had shown this action to Jim and Grotowski, they told me they had understood nothing. It appeared they had not really believed so much either. The "individual structure" was too short, I had not taken the time needed to tell the story. Now I was rushing. This time, however, Grotowski dealt with me softly. Through questions, he slowly tried to understand what was blocking me. He asked about the story I was trying to tell. I told him the content of the dream, and remarked that I had remembered the dream after reading one of the two fragments of the ancient text which I had chosen. "Ah," he said, "maybe this can work. Maybe there is something here." But I was going about it in all the wrong way.

From our discussion, it began to become clear to me that I should not pump. I should not try to fill a symbol with some kind of epic emotion. I should understand that physical actions meant to do, simply to do without adding anything. Don't make it more intense. Know what you are doing – and do it. It seemed to me, then, that the subject of my "individual structure" had some possibility; the problem lay in my approach. I should just

60

remember what Stanislavski had said: "We cannot remember feelings and fix them. We can just remember the line of physical actions. . ."[15]

These concepts began to become more clear intellectually, but many of the bad habits I had developed were tough to break. When I sang, for example, I manipulated my voice: my mind sang, not the flow of my body. This especially blocked me in the work on the Haitian songs, in which my body should sing. This mental manipulation led to a forced voice, and to self-observation which causes a half-closing of the larynx; as a result, my voice often tired easily. Another bad habit, difficult to break, was the same incorrect use I repeatedly made of "symbols" in the "individual structures." I would substitute a "symbol" instead of really asking myself, What did I do in the circumstances? What – without adding anything extra – was my body's way of doing, its actual process? I was asleep in bed, and rather than reconstructing the precise transitions of physical positions during my sleep, I had just lain stiff on my back, and that should have symbolized sleeping.

I also had to begin work on the other "individual structure," for the second fragment of text that I had chosen. I based this structure on a memory from childhood in which the woman who took care of me lifted and carried me around the room. She had a large mole on her neck which I would explore visually as she carried me. I had a hidden desire to touch and even eat this mole, which I called her "raisin."

Even if this structure never arrived at a level of high quality, it was an important step for me in the work with Grotowski. Here I began to break some of the bad habits I had collected, mostly over the last two years, doing "intense" avant-garde theatre. I began to fight to work simply. I saw that my inner reactions would trust and follow along, only if my physical behavior was truthful.

Thus, for this "individual structure," I spent hours and hours trying to reconstruct the physical behavior from my memory. Endless questions were asked. Which muscles of my body were tensed as she lifted me? How did my body rest in her arms? Did I try to touch her mole? What was I looking at in the room as she carried me? I tried to remember everything on the walls, the paintings, where they were hung . . . Each time I repeated the structure, I had to fight to see these paintings, to project them onto the space in front of me, and to see in my mind's eye their color and detail.

This work was extremely fatiguing and I continually lost concentration. In these moments Jim, who was watching, inevitably stopped me and had me repeat, again and again; until I had acted precisely, he believed what I was doing, and there was a sense of truth with no little plus.

I had great difficulty in actually seeing the room from my memory and projecting it onto the space in which we were working. I was reconstructing being carried without someone to carry me, and this put a lot of pressure on my stomach muscles which supported the rest of my body. After some time in rehearsal, my mind would often start complaining about the physical fatigue. Then, Jim would stop me and say that for some moments I had not been present while doing my line of actions. There were hundreds of things that might distract my concentration; the complaining mind was just one of them. It became clear that a person who watched with an attentive eye could recognize every moment in which I was not present. My series of actions and thoughts therefore had to be completely structured, in order that I might follow them from one little action to the next, without any holes in between. I saw immediately that my ability to concentrate was very weak. My mind almost always strayed; to be present and simply doing my line of actions was a constant struggle. I remember having the sensation that elaborating this structure was like trying to wade through mud up to my waist.

As I rehearsed this "individual structure" with Jim, who was very persistent, I began to become more familiar with my line of physical actions. Doing them truthfully, however, still remained a struggle. Often, and especially when singing, a voice would speak in me saying that my work was not intense enough, a negative voice that would repeat: "What you are doing is nothing." Then I would push, and lose the sense of truth. Jim would immediately catch this. After long work, however, this "individual structure" became more truthful and Jim even included it in a small montage to show Grotowski.

After having seen it, Grotowski spoke to us about what he said Stanislavski called a "truthy." Grotowski said that my "individual structure" was becoming much more truthful, but sometimes simple truth was not enough. As you watched, you could say,

"Yes, I believe, something is true – but so what." You were seeing a "truthy." Normally this meant that the subject of the "individual structure" did not deeply touch the actor. I was working around the wrong event. Grotowski suggested that I throw everything out and start from zero, searching for the subject that would be more than a "truthy." This change of subject was not "touristic" because I changed consciously: I had been digging in the wrong place. I felt more confident now that I had begun to work a little more truthfully.

I started to construct a draft of a new "individual structure" around a childhood memory of discovering that my hair was different, curly and African, whereas that of my mother was straight. I remember that Grotowski thought this subject might bear some possibility, but we never carried this "individual structure" very far. At the time I did not know why. A few years later he told me we had stopped working on this "individual structure" because the problem had been resolved. Before, I had not completely accepted my African aspect, but after, I began to accept it totally, and there was no more reason to work on this "structure": the question had been resolved.

Led by Jim, three members of the "performance team" including myself, then began to elaborate different drafts as cowboys. We made a draft in which the cowboys drive the cattle across a raging river. Here with our bodies we had to discover the physicality of riding a fast horse, circling the cows in order to form the herd and drive them across the river. This became like a "dancing" of actions. We had to move, to almost "be dancing the horse" while accomplishing the actions of the rider. We also tried to discover the cowboy's ways of calling to the cattle. In another draft the cowboys were around the campfire. One of us sat close to the fire, another played the harmonica, and I did what I imagined to be a real cowboy dance to the music of the harmonica. To help us find the cowboys, we used hats and ponchos.

As the structuration of the "Main *Action*" evolved, different moments of the "cowboy drafts" were kept. Grotowski had seen our drafts, and said, for example, that there was some possibility in my cowboy dance near the campfire. I then worked on this separately. Later, in the montage of the "Main *Action*," he inserted this dance into the structure in a specific relation with someone else's different line of actions. I had to keep the same dance with its intention, but now the situation around me had changed. For a person watching, my dance would have a specific meaning because of its context, because of the surrounding actions, and the montage. This, however, was not my concern. I was to look for my original dance with its intentions. A witness would receive a pre-constructed story from the montage, and would not even suspect that our original association had been cowboys.

At this point in the structuring of the "Main *Action*," two elements on which I had worked in those drafts were kept: the ride, and the dance of the cowboy. Some of the other actors' elements as cowboys were also kept and utilized in different moments in that version of the "Main *Action*." It should be noted that the "Main *Action*" was always evolving until its final version. The process took one year, but already after two months we had structured an entire version on which we worked every day. This structure would be changed and transformed all along the way, until we arrived at the final version. From a very early stage, we were working in precise structures, and nothing from these structures would be thrown away until something more essential had been found. No "marking" was allowed: yes, in some moments we would work technically, just coldly – for example, to memorize positioning in the space – but normally every time we worked on the "Main *Action*" or a fragment of it, we had to do so fully.

In the final version of the "Main *Action*," there was a sequence in which I had a series of actions which had been created similarly to our way of working on "individual structures." With Jim's help, I had made an "individual structure" around a memory from my childhood, in which, while I had been sleeping, I heard my father screaming with pain in another room. I arrived to find him having excruciating hip pain. I massaged his hip. I had never before seen my father so helpless. At this point in my development, I had realized that to do something in an "individual structure" meant, simply, to do it. I remembered all of the physical behavior connected to this memory: What was the sudden change of my body's position when I was awakened by his screams? What was my first reaction? How quickly did I run to the room where he was? Then, I also tried to remember exactly how he was lying, what he said to me when I arrived, the color of his voice, how I was listening, and then in what way I rubbed his hip (which in my "individual structure" I did with him imaginarily before me). This gave me my line of physical actions, the score I had to follow.

One of the differences between Stanislavski's and Grotowski's use of physical actions lies in the technique of montage. All of my associations and actions revolved around this personal event, and that was my secret. No one who watched us do the "Main *Action*" would ever know that: they, by means of the complete montage, would receive an entirely different story. While I followed my series of physical actions related to my father, next to me an actress followed another, completely different: *her own personal story*. But, because of the precise coordination in timing and rhythm of some of our actions, and because of the proximity of her and myself, a person looking would perceive our actions as being interrelated. They would see one story which had to do with the two of us together, when in reality we were following two *completely different lines of associations and actions*, which were separate. The actress did not know the memories on which I was working, and I did not know the ones on which she was working.

From the work on this "individual structure," I discovered in practice that I should not tamper with the emotions at all. I should not even worry about them. The key to physical actions lies in the body's process. I should simply do what I was doing, and each time I repeated the "individual structure," remember more and more precisely the way in which I had done what I had done. Let the emotions be. I knelt down like this. My father was lying like this. I reach out to him and my hands were curving like this. I touched him. To massage him I have to press with my hands in a specific way. If I feel nothing, I feel nothing. My emotions are free. I would try to remember anew this *way of doing* each time I executed this "individual structure" in the "Main *Action*."

This "individual structure" was not an extraordinary action, but rather a stepping stone, an exercise. I began to understand in practice that: "The 'small truth' of physical actions stirs the 'great truth' of thoughts, emotions, experiences, and a 'small untruth' of physical actions gives birth to a 'great untruth' in the region of emotions, thoughts and imagination."[16]

I remember a pivotal work session that took place at this point. Grotowski was watching the "Main *Action*." There was a part

65

of my structure in which I walked, carrying an object to someone. Grotowski suddenly stopped us and said to me, "Yes, something is there." I was stunned – I had just been walking very simply, nothing special. But he said, "No, there was something there, true. Intention ... you were walking for someone." He asked me to remember my association linked to that moment. I should not tell it to him but write it down as exactly as I could. I took my notebook and wrote down my association.

I had walked in that way when I was bringing a present to my father in the hospital. The nurses had said I was too young to be allowed into the hospital alone, but I did not give up: now I was walking through the hospital to my father's room. I wrote down this memory.

In that walk Grotowski had seen the seeds of something that I could not yet even sense. He said it was the seeds of "organicity." Although I did not know exactly what that meant, I understood it to mean not forced, something natural, in the way that a cat's movements are natural. If I observe a cat, I notice that all of its movements are in their place, its body thinks for itself. In the cat there is no *discursive* mind to block immediate organic reaction, to get in the way. Organicity can also be in a man, but it is almost always blocked by a mind that is not doing its job, a mind that tries to conduct the body, thinking quickly and telling the body what to do and how. Such interference often results in a staccato and broken way of moving. But if you watch a cat, you see that all its movements are fluid and connected, even the fast ones. In order for a man to arrive at such organicity, either his mind must learn the right way to be passive, or learn to occupy itself only with its own task, getting out of the way so that the body can think for itself. Grotowski states:

"Organicity: it is also a term of Stanislavski. What is organicity? It is to live in agreement with natural laws, but on a primary level. One mustn't forget, our body is an animal. I am not saying: we are animals, I say: our body is an animal. Organicity is linked to a *child-aspect*. The child is almost always organic. Organicity is something which one has more of when one is young, less of as one gets older. Obviously, it is possible to prolong the life of organicity by fighting against acquired habits, against the training

66

of common life, breaking, eliminating the clichés of behavior. And, before the complex reaction, returning to the reaction which was primary."[17]

I was surprised that Grotowski had noted the possibility of organicity in so simple a walk. Here was no high revelation, I was just walking. This walk became part of the "Main *Action*": I would walk with two other men behind me. But every time I did so, I was to remember how I walked for my father in the hospital. I should not remember my feeling, but the way in which I had done it, and for whom. It was essential that in this moment I remember my intention: *for whom* I was walking. Earlier on, I was always making the mistake of concentrating on the emotional experience. I would create a symbol for what the moment had been, and then try to pump into that form/symbol the original emotional intensity. But in this walk, I had to concentrate on *how* I did it, on the precise way of walking, and for whom. I was arriving to my father in the hospital to bring him the present, I had just overcome the nurses and I walked like this . . . I should *not try to feel* proud. That I cannot do, but I can ask myself: *in that moment when I was proud, how did I walk?* I began to understand in practice what Stanislavski meant when he said, "Do not speak to me about feeling. We cannot set feeling; we can only set physical action."[18]

The "Main *Action*" was beginning to mature. Grotowski started to work separately with two of the actors (Jairo Cuesta and Pablo Jimenez). They were making a mini-structure which they did not show us for some weeks. When I saw it for the first time, I was struck by its clarity. I saw that they were not "acting" at all, they were just doing certain tasks. The key lay in truthfully doing. Don't act, do. Shortly thereafter, I joined Jairo and Pablo, and, working in this trio, developed the main motive of my role in the "Main *Action*."

The story of the "Main *Action*" began to become clear, through its montage, as the journey of a young man (in my association, the journey toward manhood or initiation), in which you see him overcome certain tests.

I will now try to analyze the wrong functioning of my inner processes, a functioning which around this time began to change. It seems, one part of myself was always trying to do the job of another: there was no inner order. When, for example, I was trying to discover a way of dancing, my mind would be telling my body what to do, constantly interrupting, saying: "No, not like that. Like this!" There could be no authentic reaction, I was always in delay because the body was tripping over the mind. My body was not so innocent either: it would spend an enormous quantity of its own energy trying to pump the emotions; in other words, trying to effect my emotional state by changing the rhythm of breathing, or creating muscular tension in order to stimulate "symptoms" of intensity. The emotions were not allowed to react naturally to my line of actions. Each mechanism was trying to do the job of another, without doing it well. All this inner confusion, like a huge knot, interrupted creative flow.

It became clear to me that there probably existed the possibility of developing a right functioning, where each mechanism, keeping its place, helped the whole. For example, the body would look to remember its process, the mind would either speak "Yes," to encourage the body, or evoke some precise memory or image that might help the body in its search. The emotions, then, left alone, might become less afraid to react to that which the body and mind were doing. In other words, the body and mind would accomplish their own individual tasks, giving room for the emotions to react naturally.

At this point a little bit of order began to crystallize. The first factor of order was, in my case – and this can be different for actors of different types – the body. Its organic stream began to speak strongly enough that the mind could no longer block it or so easily get in its way. The mind also began to learn at which moment to be passive, or to speak positively, in order to help unblock the body's process, guarding, at the same time that the structure would be maintained. In other words, the mind started to learn that it was not the unique ruler, that the body also has *its own way of thinking*, if the mind would just let the body do its job. As my mind started to learn to be more passive, my body had an open field in which to be active; and because it had been cramped in a chair for so long in our so-called educational system, when it found an open channel it came forward. It had been truly starved for its field of activity. In this moment Grotowski started to see possibility in me, and worked with me to nourish it.

A new period in our work began. So far, I had been trying to structure a piece starting uniquely from my mind. Now, I listened to the body, letting it discover the stream of actions that it needed. And the body, activated, began to find its natural and unforced way, its organicity.

Grotowski here remarked that now we should not structure quickly. Now we must recognize that some wild animal had come into the space with its organicity. It should not be trapped into the structure too soon, or we might just limit its natural drive. The animal should arrive at its natural drive, and the director should know the precise moment at which to tighten the structure, and the precise way in which he must encircle the wild animal in order not to frighten it away.

He would always speak of these moments as moments of "grace"; in which sources began to activate, deep resources in a person, when each of their movements becomes as if surrounded in lightness. When "grace" carries, Grotowski said, then don't interrupt. That is not the moment to structure, to work on physical actions, not yet the moment to fix the actions, because if you do, you risk turning the emerging unknown into the known. You might just kill this something which is appearing. For this reason he began to work with me personally.

Grotowski always knew exactly when to step in and demand structure. Like an expert hunter, the director must feel the actor's process from within, through his own intuition, and know . . . now, structure! The moment to tighten the structure is the instant the unknown has fully appeared, right before it begins to lose its initial force: then you must tighten. At this level the craft becomes extremely delicate, like riding a wild animal: you should know when to pull the reins ("the structure"), and when to let them go, so that the animal can run free. At a certain point, the "Main *Action*" became a structure in which this discovery might run free.

The structure of the "Main *Action*" was never a perfected one: we worked on it for a year and arrived at a "stage in the work" which was like a large accomplished draft. When, toward the end of that year, the final version was completed, various persons visited the Objective Drama Program and saw us doing this "*Action*." I suppose that from the montage they saw the story of a young man, a "native boy" (myself), who, in a tribal or village situation, goes through a rite of passage into manhood. But what *they* might have seen was not my concern.

Much earlier that year, suddenly from one day to the next,

I had understood my mistakes. The point actually arrived when Jim had to come to me and say there were certain things that I simply must not do: I should not make noise when in movement, I should not have heavy breathing, I should not lose contact with my partners, etc. .... He listed point by point the specific things I should not do. The next day, we did the "Main *Action*." The following afternoon, Jim invited me to lunch, and said that Grotowski had asked him to tell me that I had succeeded in breaking absolutely all the rules. Then, it dawned on me: my participation in the group was on the line. In that instant – it completely sunk in – I understood the type of active attention I would have to keep in order not to commit what were already coming to be called "Thomas' crimes." These crimes were even listed on a sheet of paper so that I could study what *I should not do*. Well, evidently the next time we did the "Main *Action*," I did not break the rules. I stuck to my line of physical actions with the precise attention required.

On the whole, the "Main *Action*" served as a place for that newly discovered organicity to find itself. Yet, as I would later see, the demand for precision at that time was relatively minimal. The stream was flowing by itself, some source had been touched, and it was not the time to make the stream more narrow.

After we stopped working on the "Main *Action*," Grotowski told me how amateur it actually was. I had difficulty believing him, because it was the most precise professional performance structure I had ever worked in. Only later would I learn by experience that the "Main *Action*" was indeed structured in "large links" compared with how tightly structured a piece might become.

The end of that year saw great growth in my personal work with Grotowski. The exact moment he took an active interest in my development is very clear in my memory. From one day to the next, with no hesitation, it was as if he made a conscious decision to help me. Like the tusks of the elephant: once they've come out, they don't go back. From that point on, such was his interest and support.

He asked me to become his assistant and we transferred to Pontedera, Italy where, the following year (1986), we would found the Workcenter of Jerzy Grotowski.

AT THE WORKCENTER OF
JERZY GROTOWSKI

When we arrived in Italy in 1986, I was one of Grotowski's three assistants. Still, the responsibility was enormous: we would have to form the group, the practical team from the very beginning. At this point, Grotowski had already begun to turn his attention toward what he now considers to be the final phase of his life's research. That year we began what can be viewed as the preparation for this eventual final phase. On one level, his intentions in this period paradoxically coincide with those which Stanislavski held in the final period of his life. Grotowski himself has observed:

> "At the end of his life Stanislavski addressed the actors who assembled around him to work on *Tartuffe*, in the following spirit:
>
> I want to transmit to you the technique of work, and only the technique of work. We are not going to do a premiere, we are just going to work to understand what the technique of work is."[19]

Our first task was to find the group members. In my naïveté, I supposed we would easily find gifted artists, persons with perfected techniques of acting and especially singing, indispensable for the work with Grotowski. I was mistaken; in finding the right persons we encountered great difficulties.

Our work had special stipulations. We had no money to pay the participants; they would have to pay their own living expenses and, with the schedule often lasting from ten to twelve hours a day, the participants would have no time for an outside job. Further, we would never do a public performance, which might be difficult for some to accept. The candidates would have to be ready, like the actors around Stanislavski at the end of his life, to work not for a premiere, but for the work in itself. Only a very unique and committed person could be right for such a work: someone who could practically set aside all "normal life" concerns for a substantial period of time. Nothing of value could have been taught or learned in a short workshop, and, in fact, it actually took an entire year of intense work with someone even to see if something was possible. Therefore, almost everyone participating at the Workcenter was asked to be ready to stay a minimum of one year.

Upon arrival in Italy, we held selections for candidates from many countries, and for Grotowski's assistants, the learning intensified. We were to lead virtually everything alone. Each of us had to propose how the selection might be run, tell what he thought he could do with the candidates, and, if Grotowski approved, then conduct this work with them. We had to build the work, and Grotowski, like the experienced grandfather, watched us make mistakes and would help us out of every trap into which we fell, making sure we clearly understood where we had gone off track.

Concerning what each of the assistants *thought* he could do, Grotowski was very explicit. He ruthlessly attacked our suggestions if someone proposed to lead a work for which he was not qualified. If one of us proposed to lead the songs, for example, the immediate question was: What is the level of your mastery of these songs? Grotowski was trying to find the right place for each of us. Many times he quoted Napoleon as having said: The greatest sin is when a man is *not on his place*; when a man is destined to be a general, and instead is a corporal, or when someone who truly has the capacities of a corporal, takes the place of a general. From our first discussions with Grotowski in Pontedera, it became clear to me that in terms of technique, we assistants practically did not have a leg to stand on. He was surely aware of this and through these conversations made us aware of it, letting us discover it logically by ourselves.

Grotowski said that in such a situation there was only one recourse: kamikaze. This strategy, he said, can function only one time, because it is so hard. But now, in order to defend our presence as assistants, it was our only chance. This kamikaze attitude left a lot of tension in some of the persons who had participated in these first selections. They seemed to get the impression that we were all crazy, working inflexibly, with no compassion. They did not know, however, that our working so hard was in reality a test for us. Endurance was our only way to fight in the moment; we tested ourselves to the limit.

In the work at Irvine, I had been protected, but now it was just the opposite. This first selection was open battle, and soon thereafter we held many more selections, working with hundreds of candidates. I expected most of them to be immensely qualified, but it became clear that any work we might achieve, we would have to construct from zero.

Before the selections began, we assistants had to determine what each of us could lead with the participants. After a number of trials, we arrived at the following basic division of responsibilities: I would lead the work on the ancient songs (in a first period Haitian, and later African and Afro-Caribbean); develop a physical training with the participants; lead them in "Games in movement," half improvised/half structured (derived from the initial version of "Watching" in Irvine); and introduce them to the basics of "Motions." One of my colleagues would work mainly on individual "Acting propositions" of the participants, and the other would help in the work on "Games in movement," "Motions," and the physical training. Grotowski oversaw all of the work, analyzing it privately with the assistants and publicly with the candidates, when necessary. As the time to select the candidates for the group arrived, we assistants proposed to Grotowski, individually, by secret ballot, our set of candidates or – as was more often the case – candidate. Grotowski then had the final decision; but he very rarely chose someone who we had not proposed ourselves.

In this first selection, I was not focusing on elements of work which demanded a practical knowledge of physical actions. I was still in a period of development in which Grotowski was letting my "horse" run. I led the elements of work in which I could improvise spontaneously *within a structure*. In these elements, such as training and "Games in movement," the need for a score of physical actions did not come into play. I was still concentrating on the source, working at the root where the unknown might appear. The elements I conducted at that moment, therefore, did not require the pinpoint precision necessary in the final structuring of a piece. There were, however, in these first selections, moments in which I worked on "Acting propositions" with candidates; and there, I immediately confronted the difficulty of structuring a piece as director. The difference became clear to me between physical actions on one side; and activities, movements, symptoms (for instance, to blush), and gestures on the other.

One day I was working with several candidates at the same time: each worked individually but – for lack of space – all in the same room, preparing "Acting propositions" related to a song. Each was to structure an individual piece around an old song which they remembered hearing as a child. It was easy for me to see that some of these propositions were working and others not, but why? For example, one young actor chose walking on a tightrope; in his "Acting proposition" you saw that he was singing a song while pretending to walk on a tightrope. These were activities, not actions: it did not have a *why*, a *for whom*, or an *against whom*.

Grotowski always pointed out the difference between physical actions on one side and activities, movements, gestures, and symptoms on the other; saying that the mistaking of the latter for the former is one of the elementary errors one makes when trying to work according to Stanislavski's "method of physical actions." We often made such confusions when preparing "Acting propositions" for him; mistaking, for example, *activities* for actions. In his conference at Santarcangelo in 1988, Grotowski stated:

"What we must immediately understand is that which physical actions *are not*. For example: they are not activities. Activities in the sense: to clean the floor, wash the dishes, smoke the pipe. These are not physical actions, they are activities. And where people think to work according to the 'method of physical actions,' they all the time make this confusion. The directors who work on physical actions often make the actors do a lot of floor-cleaning and dishwashing on stage. But an activity can *become* a physical action. For example, you ask me a very embarrassing question (as is usually the case), so, you ask me this question and I stall for time. I begin then to solidly prepare my pipe. Now my activity becomes a physical action, because it becomes my weapon: 'Yes I am actually very busy, I must

74

prepare my pipe, clean it, light it, afterwards I will respond to you . . .' "[20]

Here Grotowski points out the difference between activities and physical actions. In our selections there were very few people who would immediately construct a proposition along the line of physical actions. Most often, someone would sing the song while executing some activity. With the right questions and given the specific circumstance, however, even some of these activities could be transformed into actions. But the actor I mentioned before was constructing his "Acting proposition" like most of the candidates, with activities. He was singing his song while pretending to walk on a tightrope. *Activities are not actions.* Grotowski often repeated this indication.

Analyzing the *difference between physical actions and gestures,* Grotowski said:

"Another misunderstanding about physical actions is that they are gestures. Actors like to make many gestures because they suppose it is their craft. There also exist professional gestures, gestures of priests, for example, as in my case sometimes . . . I am very sacramental . . . But they are gestures, they are not actions. [. . .]

Now, what is a gesture, if we look from the outside? How to easily recognize a gesture? Most often a gesture is a *peripheral* movement of the body, a gesture is not born from the inside of the body, but from the periphery (the hands and the face)."[21]

"There is a big difference between the peasant who works with his hands and the man of the city who never worked with his hands. The latter has the tendency to make gestures rather than actions. We can say: he is a man alive in the head. But he is often not alive, he is not organic. In reality, it is because he makes gestures and not actions. Observe: the man of the city who has the tendency to make gestures, gives his hand to another like this [Grotowski gives his hand starting from the hand]. The peasants go from the inside of the body, like this [Grotowski gives his hand starting from the inside of the body through the arm]. It is a very big difference (I borrow this observation from a Polish actor of peasant origins)."[22]

75

Describing the *difference between movements and physical actions*, Grotowski in his analysis added:

"It is easy to confuse physical actions with movements. If I am walking toward the door, it is not an action but a movement. But if I am walking toward the door to contest 'your stupid questions,' to threaten you that I will break up the conference, there will be a cycle of little actions and not just a movement. This cycle of little actions will be related to my contact with you, my way of perceiving your reactions; when walking toward the door, I will still keep some 'controlling look' toward you (or I will listen) to know if my threat is working. So it will not be a walk as movement, but something much more complex around the fact of walking. The mistake of many directors and actors is to fix the movement instead of the whole cycle of little actions (actions, reactions, points of contact) which simply appears *in the situation* of the movement."[23]

In this first selection, there was another young actor, F., who was working on an "Acting proposition" approaching the right use of physical actions. The story was related to his father. One night his father had come home drunk from the bar, singing until he fell down and passed out. F., with his own body, started to reconstruct the physical behavior of his father, remembering exactly what his father had been doing, reconstructing the logical line of his physical actions. First, F. tried to remember the physical behavior in the given circumstances. He walked into the house. How did he walk? He was heavy. In what way was he heavy? Where was he looking? He was looking at the floor. Why was he looking at the floor? Where was the heaviness located in his body? What was the song he was singing? And why this song? What was his way of singing? Which body resonator was his voice placed in, and why? Why did he get drunk?

F., in his "Acting proposition" around the memory of his father, was constructing the truthful line of physical behavior by remembering exactly what his father had done. He approached a discovery of the inner desires of his father, since true physical actions are always linked to desires or wishes. In the work of F., I began to see his father. I was not seeing F. "play" his father, but rather execute the actions of his father, simply.

Through him I started to see another person: F. was still there, but it was as if another person arrived through him.

This is not the same as Stanislavski's work on character. Stanislavski centered his research on *building a character* within the story and the given circumstances of a theatre text. The actor would ask himself: What is the logical line of physical actions that I would do if I were in the circumstances of *this character*? In the work of Grotowski, however – for example in his work with the Laboratory Theatre – the actors did not *look* for characters. The characters appeared rather in the mind of the spectator because of the montage (in the performance and in the role). Grotowski stressed this aspect many times when speaking about the work of Ryszard Cieslak in *The Constant Prince*. Cieslak basically worked not on the character of Calderon's tragedy, but on personal memories related to an important event of his life.

In this period of our work with Grotowski, we also created actions directly with personal memories. Through acting you might be remembering some moment in your life, or someone close to you, or a concrete event from your fantasy that never happened, that you always wished had happened. You might construct, then, the structure through physical actions. You would ask: What did I do in the circumstances of this memory? Or: What precisely would be my line of physical behavior if this fantasy had actually happened? The emphasis being not on the creation of a character, but on the formation of a personal structure in which the person doing might approach some axis of discovery. All this, then, should be structured and repeatable.

At work with Grotowski in Irvine, and later in Italy, we were looking for neither the character nor the *non-character*. Grotowski describes one aspect of our work as follows:

"One access to the creative way consists of discovering in yourself an ancient corporality to which you are bound by a strong ancestral relation. So you are neither in the character nor in the non-character. Starting from details, you can discover in you somebody other – your grandfather, your mother. A photo, a memory of wrinkles, the distant echo of a color of the voice enable you to reconstruct a corporality. First, the corporality of somebody known, and then more and more distant, the corporality

of the unknown one, the ancestor. Is this corporality literally as it was? Maybe not literally – but yet as it might
have been. You can arrive very far back, as if your memory
awakens. This is a phenomenon of reminiscence, as if you
recall the Performer of primal ritual. Each time I discover
something, I have the feeling that it is what I recall.
Discoveries are behind us and we must journey back to
reach them.

With the breakthrough – as in the return of an exile –
can one touch something which is no longer linked to
origins but – if I dare say – to *the origin*?"[24]

With Stanislavski, the "method of physical actions" was a
means for his actors to create "a real life," a "realistic" life in
performance. For Grotowski, rather, the work on physical actions
was a tool to find this "something" in which there would be a
personal discovery for the one doing. For both Stanislavski and
Grotowski physical actions were a means, but their ends were
different.

After the initial selections, we decided to choose a provisory
group, and conduct a workshop with them for a longer period,
before making the final decision as to who should stay in the
group. In this workshop, I began to work on an "Acting proposition" with a young man, B., who would later become a key
member in the group I now lead, "Downstairs Group."

B. tried to do an "Acting proposition" in which he was singing
an old Italian song. When the text of the song spoke of a cow,
B. made a cow with his body. When the song spoke of the moon,
B. looked up to the moon. He was making the mistake of illus-
trating the song. His "Acting proposition" became a string
of indications that copied what the song said. In this way the
proposition would never work. It became white on white; no
contrast.

I worked with B. in what might be considered the director's
position, helping him from the outside. I asked him what his
personal memories around this song were, and he told me he
had sung it as a child. I asked him where and in what circumstances. We started to construct his "Acting proposition" around
a childhood memory from the age of seven. One of the first
things we spoke about were his shoes. He needed to find the

physicality of a seven-year-old, and it seemed important that he find the right shoes. They needed to be a little too big for him. He felt such shoes might help him rediscover his particular way of walking as a child. Once he had found the shoes, he started to experiment, looking for the different ways in which he used to walk. He entered a game of remembering. I took close note of anything he came up with. I was attentive to notice the moments when something subtle in him changed. As soon as his body really remembered his young way of walking, I would see something in him react: he became lighter, younger, actually like a child playing. In this way we captured and then structured his ways of walking. We had to elaborate them technically until his body had memorized them. He then recalled that when he had sung this song as a child, he had been alone playing in one of the grain silos. I asked him to remember and recreate this way of playing. He did an improvisation to remember physically the games he used to play. I noted the games that had a particularly strong effect on him: in one, he sang the song down a shaft to create an echo; in another, he entered the grain silo, for him a magic place, in a special way. He discovered a box full of old objects. He spun on the heels of his shoes, which led him to stick his finger in some unknown substance.

I worked with B. until he found the line of actions that seemed to effect him most. From these games and discoveries in his magic place, we created a small piece, his "Acting proposition." We worked on this for some time, and I felt good because we had found the way to structure not activities, but actions. We had constructed his line of physical actions around a specific childhood memory.

Grotowski saw this work as positive, but finally he said we had reached the highest point possible with that material. So we stopped working on that proposition and went on to other pieces. That "Acting proposition," however, had been a step ahead for the understanding of both B. and myself in the work on physical actions. B. had the practical possibility to see that physical actions did not mean to illustrate the activities spoken about in a song, and I began to see how a *line* of actions could be constructed by linking together different, smaller series of already found physical actions, in order to create a montage that was understandable and simple, and that could give to the person doing a certain potentiality of discovery.

There was an actress who worked with us in this first workshop, of whom Grotowski said, "She already understands physical actions." After having seen one of her "Acting propositions," Grotowski told me that she had craft: this actress had structured her line of physical actions so clearly that he could follow every one of her associations. At the time I was not so impressed by her "Acting proposition," it seemed too simple. Grotowski was impressed, it seemed, by her clarity and ability to compose. This young woman was gifted in the realm of composition.

I have arrived at the point in my narrative where I should speak a little about different types of actors, and the different ways that physical actions might work for them.

When I met this young woman, I began to see that there exist different types of actors. One type of actor, like this young woman, is more centered in the mind, as if her dominion is strongly located in the logical mind. Often this kind of actor will work well with physical actions when *as the first step* they construct the proposition. They approach acting from the logical mind, first asking themselves, what did they, or would they do in the circumstances. They often construct a score and memorize the logical sequence of actions even before they do any physical actions. The danger for this type of actor is that sometimes their art, though logical, remains cold and never touches the heart; even if there is no doubt that there are actors of this type who arrive at a high level in their art.

Another type of actor is one whose line of physical actions will not be indicated first by the mind. The line of actions, when it arrives, will be more a series of very small organic impulses that comes from inside the body. The body will dictate the sequence of actions as something that it needs to do, something deeply natural for it to do. This type of actor is more centered in organicity. And if the mind of this person learns to be passive in the right way, then the flow of the impulses in their body will lead them toward a deep process. With this type of actor, the structure should be shaped later. Their mind will understand, only *after* the birth of their line of actions, what the actual memory was. In this case, first the body remembers and after the mind will say, "Ah, that is what I was doing at that time"; but first the body has remembered. Then this stream of impulses should be linked to the stream of associations already caught. The danger for this type of actor is that they can remain dilet-

80

tante, and though their work in the moment of improvisation is warm and spontaneous, they may never master the ability to work within a precise structure and repeat a sequence of actions with complete accuracy.

In both these examples of different types of actors, a logical score of physical actions is arrived at, but the way of arrival and the dangers along the way are different. In reality, on the highest level, the actor centered more in the mind arrives at organicity through composition, and the actor centered more in the body arrives at composition through organicity; both passing through the work on physical actions.

These are just two of the possibilities; of course, there exist many others.

One danger for each type of actor is that the actions, after they are structured, "die," and what were once physical actions become empty movements or gestures. This is the biggest danger and must be fought actively all along the way. One must remember: What was I doing and to whom? Or even, For whom? This *for whom* or *to whom* is key.

When a line of physical actions "dies," one possible cause is that the actor has forgotten the contact with his partner. After many repetitions, the actor already feels sure of what his partner will do, so he is no longer attentive to him. He merely repeats his own score blindly, and his actions lose their original life. This problem can be overcome if the actor remembers in what way he is trying to effect his partner. The partner will each day be a little different, and if you are truly attentive to your partner, you will have to adjust each time to his slightly different way of doing, without breaking your own line of physical actions. From this subtle adjustment comes the fresh life of a given moment in an action. This is the *main* strategy, Grotowski said, to keep a line of actions from falling into the "general." We should every time *keep contact with our partner*.

This adjustment to the partner within a fixed line of actions is what Stanislavski and Grotowski considered true spontaneity. High-level spontaneity can arrive *only in a piece which is structured*. At that point the actors can find freedom inside their structure, freedom not to change their line of actions, but to adjust slightly in reaction to one another (and to everything around), still keeping the same intentions and the same *line of actions*. This is some kind of subtle improvisation in which the structure is tight, and of course perfectly memorized. Grotowski stated: "Spontaneity is impossible without structure. Rigor is necessary to have spontaneity."[25] He continued: "According to Stanislavski: actions which are absorbed (learned, memorized) completely, only these can become free. [...] Here is the rule: 'What to do next?' – *is* the paralysis. *'What to do next?'* This is the question that makes all spontaneity impossible."[26]

When I saw this young woman work, I realized there were different types of actors. She had one approach and I another. To work with her I could not just repeat how I worked with myself, or even see my own process in her. She was like a completely different animal which called for a completely different strategy. Grotowski was aware of this and praised her for her special quality. She had exactly what we assistants lacked: the technique of composition. Grotowski said that among all of us working with him at the Workcenter, this actress was the only one who knew how to structure a piece, and he suggested that we assistants steal her secret.

One year later, in 1987, during a conference held in Florence on the Workcenter of Jerzy Grotowski, Peter Brook said:

"... the man who dreams of a role in life: *becoming an actor*, can, in a perfectly natural way feel that his duty is to go straight towards the world of the theatre. But he may also feel something else, he may feel that all this gift, all this love is an opening towards another understanding; and he may feel that he can't find this understanding except through personal work with a master ..."[27]

When it was a question of accepting this actress or not, Grotowski said that she *should not* be accepted, using an argument similar to the one appearing in the words of Peter Brook just quoted. This actress, Grotowski said, is not destined to look through her acting directly for some inner discoveries, but now to go into the big world of theatre, with the brilliant lights of the stage and the life around. To stay with us, he said, will be good neither for her nor for us.

BEGINNING STAGES

For the time being, we had finished selections, though we would conduct others in the future almost every year. We now worked with a preliminarily stable group, taking time to see who really were the right persons for this work.

During this period, in an attempt to steal this actress's compositional skill, I structured a piece in a very different way. I tried to use a composition technique similar to that in Western music. Grotowski's proposition had been to create a "storm of human symptoms." I did not really know what "symptoms" were. I only knew that this time we should not look for physical actions, but something different. After many trials and failures, the "symptoms" turned out to be personal and distinctive sounds of human reactions. These "symptoms," when they worked, would always be linked to a strong memory of the person who reproduced them. For example, the person remembered having heard the striking way a friend had laughed, or the sound of someone's sickness who was very close, or the sound someone had made as he died, or the sound that someone made in response to that death. With these "symptoms," I was to structure a score in which the "symptoms" seemed to approach from a distance, build slowly in intensity, climax over us and then disappear; like a storm which approaches, breaks and then leaves.

First I worked with the actors, five of them, one at a time. Each was to discover a few personal "symptoms." Not actions! The body's process was always key in the alive reproduction of the sound. Often an actor would have a specific way of moving that would help him rediscover the sound. When all of the "symptoms" had been found and approved by Grotowski, I worked like a music composer, orchestrating them in a score to create the effect that they slowly arrived from a distance, climaxed over us, and then parted. I wrote a complicated score which had the "symptoms" overlapping one another. I then taught the actors the score, so that they would know exactly when to enter with each "symptom." In the end, if everything functioned, a storm of distinct human "symptoms" would arrive. We were avoiding banal symptoms such as the sound of scratching or burping, but were looking for specific sounds that the persons distinctly remembered. Most often it was important for the actor to remember not only the exact sound and its intonation, but the moment in which it had appeared: in other words, his exact memory. It would also help the actor to remember the body's reactions that had produced this sound.

Often the "symptom" would no longer be alive, having lost its specificity. Then we would have to fight against the onslaught of the "general." I would remind the actor of his memory, and search for the way that he might remember the process involved in producing the "symptom." Sometimes, however, this did not work. In these cases, Grotowski often pointed out that the original "élan" was missing.

Elan: I understood it more through Grotowski's way of saying it than through any verbal explanation. When Grotowski said "élan," the word contained a very specific quality of vocal vibration which was itself the definition. It began with a strong attack (not loud), around the middle of the word you could feel an increase in drive, some sort of inner explosion, and then it ended in a quasi-growl. Just now when I was checking to see if my description of Grotowski's way of speaking this word was accurate, I spoke it myself, trying to recreate his vocal vibration, and the dog in the courtyard, even if it was some forty yards away, reacted and began barking. This was the effect of élan. I don't have an accurate word to describe it, but it is something close to "drive," a "continuous drive."

Elan was something with which you should enter your line of physical actions. For example, when an action was first appearing, the élan would be full because the action flowed with the force and momentum of the discovery. But after some time of repetition, the action might lose something. At that moment, I might mistakenly think about emotional intensity. But no! That would be a big mistake. When Grotowski worked on an action which was in such a descending state, he would often direct us to find again the original élan of the line of actions. It was this which might be missing. If this drive could be found again, often everything would fall into place, the line of actions would begin to flow with its original force.

One day I remember Grotowski working personally with a French actress, N., who was participating in a selection. Normally in selections, he would not work personally with the candidates, but this time he did. I suppose he saw in her some strong possibility and, indeed, she became an important member of our group. He tried very rapidly to get her to structure and to keep precisely a line of small actions which she had improvised. This work was a battle: N. resisted saying she could not understand Grotowski's French. Grotowski said that the problem was not his French, and immediately switched languages, now giving her all directions in Polish, a language she could not understand at all! I was amazed. There was such élan behind his way of speaking Polish, and such lack of hesitation that she had no choice but to understand. She began to fight to execute all of his directions immediately. The session continued much better than before, despite the fact that Grotowski continued to give his directions uniquely in Polish. Elan was surely the key.

We had practically finished the work on "the storm of symptoms," and it was giving interesting results. I had tried to steal the way of working which started from construction. Grotowski said that the task was accomplished, and, afterwards, directed us toward another work.

Grotowski asked us to create "Acting propositions" around fragments of the same ancient text which had been worked on in Irvine. I chose a fragment, and first composed the song which this time seemed to come surprisingly easily. I was so enthusiastic about the melody, that during rehearsal that night I went into a room alone and sang it over and over again. Grotowski had been listening to me from another room, and afterwards made a very important comment to me about *singing mechanically*. He said that in the beginning as I sang the song, still being unsure of its melody, my way of singing was very alive; modest and alive because there was a true action: I was *searching* for the song. But the moment I thought I knew the song, I started to sing *as if I knew it*, and there was no more action, only mechanical repetition. Then the song was dead, not working. Since I thought I knew the song, I was no longer involved in an alive search.

85

"Yes," I said. "What you say is true, but the search was alive in the beginning because I was really in the process of creating the melody; but now I know the melody, the search is over." Grotowski told me that there was a way to sing in which the searching never died. Even though you knew the melody by heart and did not alter it, you always approached it like a friend whom you don't completely know: another being. You go forward into the song, asking it to reveal its secret to you. Even when you know the melody by heart, there must always be a search, like looking to meet someone. Don't treat the song as if you already know it.

I remember another occasion when Grotowski spoke of a similar phenomenon: we meet someone who becomes our friend, and we think we know him. After some time of friendship we no longer *see* him, we just look at him; every day he is before us but we no longer really see. This is because we already *think* we know him. Since we are no longer seeing, our contact with that person becomes mechanical. But, look at your friend and see, now. Not only is his face a different face every day, but he, himself, will be a slightly different person from day to day.

Grotowski was asking that I look to meet the song like someone I did not know, or someone whom I was in the process of knowing. Then in the singing there would be an active search, which would block mechanical repetition. I understood him then, and was much more careful in my approach to this song.

In those days I had an important dream about playing in the house where I lived as a child. I decided to structure my "Acting proposition" around this dream. I built the line of actions starting from the dream and memorized them. I decided in which sequences of physical actions the song would appear. After memorizing the line of actions, I quickly started to work physically in order not to lose the process of the dream still fresh in my memory.

I refined the structure in a new way, which became for me very natural: I would not stop, but would repeat the structure over and over again, now changing this, now putting one of the actions in a different place; I worked in an unbroken stream, trying to let the body remember the line of the dream. I would see that certain elements of the dream were more important than others, so I would immediately try again, eliminating one little action, or changing the order of little actions or – even –

86

associations, to see what worked best. Slowly eliminating all extraneous material, I arrived at the final version.

As I was doing this work something special took place. My colleague B. was working in the same space on *his* "Acting proposition." Not only did I have to work on and execute my own actions, but at the same time I had to be conscious of when B. wanted to sing, and give him room. I should not change my melody, but fix my pitch so that my song was in natural harmony with his. As we were working on our respective "Acting propositions" in the same room, a strong mutual attention was created between us. He was making room for me in all of the right moments, and I for him. It was as if another attention awoke in me, to take care to adjust to and not disturb B. I started to feel as if I was flying; our songs together were producing an extraordinary harmony. With my main attention on my own line of physical actions and song, and my secondary attention on B., there came in the midst of this long stream of work, an incredibly light feeling of repose, even though my structure was quite dynamic. The adjusting was on a high level: I would sense that B. needed a little more silence in a given moment, and since I could not break my flow of physical actions, I would slow down slightly to give him the time he needed.

This level of coordination was new for me. It demanded a very light and agile attention. Such coordination in this phase of our work did not often occur, but when it did, it left an uncommon sense of inner peace.

Another actor, P., entered the group. In the beginning I helped him to elaborate an "Acting proposition" so that he and I might both have a chance to work on physical actions. This work with P. proved to be both instrumental and difficult. P. was dilettante in a specific way: in an improvisation, what he did would amaze you and open your heart, his presence would be fantastically light and alive. But the moment we would try to structure his improvisation in an "Acting proposition," the life disappeared.

Once, I remember P. started to improvise, and it was extraordinary, I was just laughing and laughing. He was doing an old man he had seen in his village playing accordion. P. did not play accordion, but he would sing the part of the accordion and remember the way in which the old man's body was in contact with the instrument. When I first saw this proposition, it was so light! I really saw the old man shining through him. Then, when I asked him to repeat, his line of actions immediately became mechanical. He sang the same melody of the accordion, but the song now did not ring as before. Everything became more "general." When first done the line of actions was rich and specific, but when he tried to repeat it, the specificity evaporated.

We were faced with our common human weakness: the descent due to inner laziness. The first improvisation was effortless, P. was carried by the first impact of the memory. But when he tried to repeat, the downward pull of laziness made his actions become more and more general. This phenomenon can only be fought by persistent efforts. To master any skill, one must develop the ability to overcome and break through this inner laziness. P. would repeat the "Acting proposition," and where there had been six small actions, now there was one, larger and more "general." Initially the song had been sung with many peaks and valleys, like inner waves, but now there were none, the vibratory quality had become more flat.

Grotowski told me that when Stanislavski had analyzed this danger, he realized that when an actor knows a score of physical actions very well, in order to keep it from descending, as time passes one must break the same score down into smaller actions. Instead of letting it simplify, become more general, one should work in the opposite direction: the line of actions must be made more detailed. The more an actor repeats a line of physical actions, the more he must divide each action into smaller actions; every action becoming more complex. It is not that the actor should change his line of actions, but rather that he should discover the smaller elements within this same line of actions, so that the original line of actions becomes more detailed.

Grotowski made a demonstration. He said: if, for example, at first my action is to wait for the phone to ring, then after some time of repetition, I should break this action down into two actions: one, leaning toward the phone in expectation for it to ring; and two, a slight impulse toward the phone because I heard a sound from outside which might have been the beginning of a ring. The original action of waiting for the phone to ring is still present, but instead of it being one action, as in the beginning, it has now been broken down into two actions. What was once one action has become two, more detailed, but the action is still to wait for the phone to ring. Then, after the repetition of this more detailed score, before it begins to descend, the actor may have to find even smaller details within the same original line of actions, and then maybe even smaller details, and so on. In this way, making the same line of actions more detailed, more rich in smaller elements, the actor can fight the descent which is the inevitable adversary he confronts when repeating a performance for one, two years, or more.

We had to work to reconstruct the elements of P.'s "Acting proposition" as they had originally appeared, and then go toward even smaller elements. We asked questions. How exactly did the old man hold his accordion? What were his impulses like when he played? What was the precise "dancing" of his body? When P. would enter into an active search to remember the elements, his actions would immediately come alive again. And this is the key: he was involved in a search, he was fighting, he was looking for, trying to remember, asking how it had been. Was it like this? And then my attention as spectator was immediately drawn to him, because I saw that he was truthfully and simply *doing* something.

Many times I would remind him from the outside how he had originally done certain elements. The danger when working in this way is that I remind him of the exterior form: this might just push him to fix his "Acting proposition" in forms and not in actions. But such a strategy might also lead him to *remember* the initial line of actions. For example, I tell him that his arm was bent in a slightly different angle; in the moment of telling him this, I am conscious that I do so in the hope that his body will start to remember by itself its original doing. I indicate the form as starting data for the body to remember. It is possible that this strategy can work in some specific situations, and in others not. Grotowski many times stressed the fact that *there is no method*, there is only what works and what does not work in any individual case. If a strategy was not working, we should not guard it sanctimoniously but change it and find what will work.

This type of information about the shaping of the body, though dangerous, worked for P.; only because his body, finding its forgotten position, was then in a path toward remembering how this moment had originally been done. Often an artist will substitute superficial form for his initial line of actions in an attempt to remove discomfort. From the exterior you see that he has changed a difficult position of his body. First, when the line of actions was fully articulated, at its best level, his body was in the original, harder position. He should then remove the faulty, *easier*, positioning of the body.

I should like to stress that the indicating of exterior form may work, and if it works, the indication is useful. But one ought to take care: for the actor who has an inclination to make gestures (meaning, an actor who easily loses the original intention), this type of indication might be disastrous. Putting his mind on form, you simply push him toward his weakness: he is already formalizing the work. Grotowski states: "The fundamental thing, it seems to me, is always to precede the form by what should precede it, by a process which leads to the form."[28]

This principle was present in all aspects of our work: one should *arrive* at a form – it is related to structure and is necessary – but there is an arrival, a living process that should not be lost. In reality, on a high level, form and process are not two, but one: when the process is lived totally, the form is also apparent. But in appearance, and also to a certain extent in practice, we can speak of two aspects: through process one arrives at articulated form. Without a living process, there is just aesthetics; and living process which does not arrive at articulated form, is "soup."

P., as an actor, however, did not so much have the danger of losing intention. His danger was precisely the opposite, that of losing the form. Thus, often I had to indicate to his body its original position. Many times, remembering the form at which a physical action had arrived, helped him to remember even more precisely the original physical action.

At one moment in his "Acting proposition," P. approached a river and began to wade out into its current. Here once again his improvisation was clear and alive: I could see the river and feel its cold water. But as he repeated his line of actions, this moment descended toward pseudo-spontaneity. We had to spend much time working on details, asking ourselves: How did you touch the water? Your body was bent over? In what way? No, I don't think so, before it was a little different. What was your physical reaction when your foot hit the cold water? No, I don't believe you. You are exaggerating, what was it truthfully? Again. How large is the river? How deep? Did you roll your pants up before you went into the river? Ah, you did. In what way? The work on all of these details is absolutely essential, and only through this can one arrive at a result that is truly accomplished. This type of questioning can never stop for the actor. The moment P. thought, "Ah, now I know how I did it," he would immediately become mechanical. Something in his way of doing, in his attention, sat down and I, as witness, was no more drawn to watch him.

This work on details fatigued me terribly. I often felt as if a wave of sleep were pulling me down. This must be fought at all costs, otherwise you will – as director – simply give into *your own* laziness which really does not want you to complete anything: it would rather that you just move on to something else, easier and to the side.

Again and again I would repeat with P. his "Acting proposition," fighting to keep his search for the articulated details alive. By "search for the articulated details," I do not mean improvising new details each time, but keeping alive the search for even smaller details. In his "Acting proposition," P. should not merely repeat something he already knew, but each time remember how the accordion was singing, how the old man was moving – Was it like this, exactly? No. It was more like this? Ah, yes, that's it! Now, the vibration of the voice . . . how was it? No, more like . . . this. Yes! – So that each small element in his "Acting proposition" would be an alive search, not just dead repetition.

Through this work with P., I began to notice the subtle difference between physical actions that are alive and physical actions that have just slipped into mechanical repetition. P. greatly improved his conscious fight against descent into the "general." Grotowski had spoken to P. about aging, saying that he was in the last moment of his life in which he could still delay aging through intense physical training. Organic training was the only measure, because P. was on the border of becoming physically old. From that moment on, something in P.'s strategy changed, and through his new fight his capacities remarkably increased.

Around this time, aside from the work with the group, I began to work closely with Grotowski alone on the "Song *Action*." I worked alone with him on this "Song *Action*" for approximately one year, before others were chosen to join. By the time they entered into that *"Action,"* my score was already completely set. In this work on the "Song *Action,"* Grotowski was trying to let me rediscover the process hidden in the work on the ancient Afro-Caribbean and African songs. It was no longer on a level of realistic actions of "daily life."

The period from the first workshops with Grotowski, through the year at the Objective Drama Program, including the first phase at the Workcenter of Jerzy Grotowski, can be seen as one block of my work. After that, what I learned in this first block continued to be utilized, but the work itself entered a *completely new stage*, in which all of the main elements changed. The work of this new block is currently in progress, and is not the topic of this text.

GROTOWSKI VS. STANISLAVSKI: THE IMPULSES

I would like now to look at the difference between Stanislavski's "method of physical actions" and Grotowski's work on physical actions. Grotowski did not simply employ a technique created by Stanislavski, the situation is much more complex. Grotowski took "physical actions" forward from the point where Stanislavski stopped working because he died. One day, when speaking to me about his work on physical actions, Grotowski said: "It is not really Stanislavski's 'method of physical actions,' but what is after." It is rather a continuation.

In his work, Grotowski redefines the notion of *organicity*. For Stanislavski, "organicity" signified the natural laws of "normal" life which, by means of structure and composition, appear on the stage and become art; while for Grotowski, *organicity* indicates something like the potentiality of a current of impulses, a quasi-biological current that comes from the "inside" and goes toward the accomplishment of a precise action.

Concerning the question of *impulse* there is also a difference between Stanislavski and Grotowski. In his book, *The Work of the Actor on the Role* (*Rabota aktera nad rol'ju*), in the chapter dedicated to the *Inspector General* of Gogol, Stanislavski writes about impulse:

"I now repeat all the actions marked down in these notes and, to avoid stereotypes (given that for now there have not yet been consolidated in me truthful and productive actions), I will pass from one task to the next without executing them physically. For now I will limit myself to stimulate and reinforce the impulses interior to the action. As regards the truthful and productive actions, they are born by themselves, nature will take care of it.

Arkadij Nikolaevic tries not to move at all, but to communicate with the eyes and the facial expression."[29]

Here Stanislavski seems to suggest that the work on impulses is related to "the eyes and the facial expression": the *periphery* of the body.

Grotowski, however, speaking about impulse says:

"Before a small physical action there is an impulse. Therein lies the secret of something very difficult to grasp, because the impulse is a reaction that begins inside the body and which is visible only when it has already become a small action. The impulse is so complex that one cannot say that it is only of the corporeal domain."[30]

In his conference at Liège (1986), Grotowski analyzed the question as follows:

"And now, what is the impulse? 'In/pulse' – push from inside. Impulses precede physical actions, always. The impulses: it is as if the physical action, still almost invisible, was already born in the body. It is this, the impulse. If you know this, in preparing a role, you can work alone on the physical actions. For example, when you are on the bus, or waiting in the dressing room before going back on stage. When you do cinema you lose a quantity of time waiting; actors always wait. You can utilize all of this time. Without being perceived by the others, you can train the physical actions, and try out a composition of physical actions *staying at the level of the impulses*. This means that the physical actions do not appear yet but are already in the body, because they are 'in/pulse'. For example: in a fragment of my role I am in a garden on a bench, somebody is sitting beside me, I look at her. Now, suppose I am working on this fragment alone with an imaginary partner. Exteriorly – I am not looking at this person, who I imagine – I do only the starting point: the impulse to look at her. In the same way, I do the next starting point – the impulse to lean, to touch her hand [that which Grotowski does is almost imperceptible] – but I don't let it appear fully as an action, I am only starting. You see, I move very little, because it is *only* the pulsion of touching. But I do not exteriorize. Now, I walk, I walk,

94

... but I am always in my chair. It is like this that you can train physical actions. Moreover, your physical actions can be better rooted in your nature if you train the impulses, even more than the actions. One can say that the physical action is almost born, but it is still kept back, and in this way, in our body, we are 'placing' a right reaction (like one 'places the voice'). Before the physical action, there is the impulse, which pushes from inside the body, and we can work on this: we can find ourself on the public bus without anybody noticing anything strange, and we are all the same doing our preparation. In reality, the physical action, if not begun by an impulse, becomes something conventional, almost like gesture. When we work on the impulses, everything becomes rooted in the body."[31]

Impulse, for Grotowski, is something that pushes from "inside" the body and extends itself out toward the periphery; something very subtle, born "inside the body," and which does not come from uniquely a corporeal domain.

Regarding this question, Grotowski said to me that impulses are the morphemes of acting. When I interrupted him to ask what a morpheme is, he told me to go and look it up in the dictionary. He continued, however, to explain that a morpheme is one bit of something, a bit which is elemental. It's like a basic beat of something. And the basic beats of acting are impulses prolonged into actions.

At the end of his life, Stanislavski was conscious of the question of impulses. He speaks of the possibility that the actor may "stimulate and reinforce the impulses interior to the action," but he associated them with the periphery of the body ("the eyes and the facial expression"), which is in contradiction with Grotowski's indications. The standpoint of Grotowski is that the actor looks for an *essential current* of life; the impulses are rooted *profoundly "inside" the body* and then extend outward. This development of the work on impulse is logical if we keep in mind that Grotowski looks for the organic impulses in an unblocked body going toward a fullness which is *not* of daily life.

Grotowski once said to me that there are clues which indicate that Stanislavski saw the work on impulse as a field of further investigation. While studying in Moscow as a young director, Grotowski heard about an exercise in which Stanislavski, already

95

old, had transformed himself into a tiger only with impulses. Stanislavski almost did not move at all, but only made the *impulses* of the tiger's actions: to search for his prey, prepare to jump, attack, etc. Almost without moving, through the impulses alone, Stanislavski had transformed himself into a tiger. But Stanislavski, Grotowski said, did not have the time to really work in this direction, on impulses, because he died.

According to Grotowski, impulses are linked to the *right* tension. An impulse appears in tension. When we in-tend to do something, there is a *right* tension inside, directed outside. Grotowski touched upon the question of intention in his conference at Liège in 1986:

> "In/tension – intention. There is no intention if there is not a proper muscular mobilization. This is also part of the intention. The intention exists even at a muscular level in the body, and is linked to some objective outside you.
>
> At the end of the nineteenth century, a great Polish psychologist, Ochorowicz, who was occupied with 'paranormal phenomena,' made some studies about 'telekinetic force,' that is, the phenomena which give the impression that an object moves by itself. Ochorowicz proved that it may be not this at all. It may be that there is just in/tension in the body. For example, there is an officer who exercises his soldiers over a long period, he exercises them almost like in dressage. Finally, he asks them to gather around a table and put their fingers right under the edge of the table. And then he gives the order *to the table*, he says: 'Table, dance!' And the table begins to dance. That which happens is in/tension in the soldiers; because they *expect* the table to dance, there is muscular mobilization in their bodies and in their hands which makes the table move in the requested way. This example is very important; here, you are faced with only one aspect of intention. Usually, when the actor thinks of intentions, he thinks that it means to pump an emotional state. It is not this. Intentions are related to physical memories, to associations, to wishes, to contact with the others, but *also* to muscular in/tensions."[32]

I see a possible misunderstanding: one might understand impulses simply on the level of muscular contractions, go onto the stage and start pumping pseudo-intensity through muscular contractions. To avoid such a misunderstanding, I quote another passage in which Grotowski speaks about muscular contraction and relaxation:

"It is not at all true that the actor must just be well relaxed. Many actors make an enormous quantity of relaxation exercises. But when they are on stage, they have two fatal results. One result is that they immediately become completely contracted. Before they begin, they relax, but when they find themselves in front of a difficulty, they tense up. For others, the result is that they become like a handkerchief, asthenic, psychasthenic on the stage. The process of life is an *alternation* of contractions and decontractions. So the point is not only to contract or to decontract, but to find this river, this flow, in which *what is needed* is *contracted* and *what is not needed* is *relaxed*.

Let's take an exercise of Stanislavski: he asked an actor to take a precise position in a chair and relax those muscles which are not needed for keeping this position. It means that the muscles engaged in this position should be contracted, but those which are uselessly engaged should be relaxed. This is really important. Using the term 'élan': in the useless contractions one loses an enormous quantity of 'élan.' The actor who knows to eliminate the useless contractions can bear extraordinary efforts without being exhausted. He engages the muscular contraction there where it is really needed. Like an old craftsman who works in a continuous way, without interruption. All the time he is doing something, but slowly. Imagine that your work is a rope: you don't make staccato movements, but you let this rope of your efforts come out, slowly, all the time; because to *begin* the effort always eats much more energy than to *continue* the effort. This is also linked to the *decontraction* of muscles which are *not needed* for an action.

On the other hand, Stanislavski said that the actor, because of his stage fright, has a point in the body where the useless contractions start. For instance, certain actors contract the muscle of the forehead, another actor contracts the shoulders, another the neck, another some place lower in the back, another the legs. And if you can relax your starting point of the artificial contractions, there is the possibility that the other useless contractions will relax as well. For example, if my contractions start here, on the forehead (where the contraction appears always in my situations of stage fright), then, if I relax here, the superfluous contractions in all the body for a moment disappear. This is the decontraction aspect. But now let's take the contraction aspect. Her! [Grotowski indicates with determination someone among the public.] You see – this requires that I contract the arm and the hand. It cannot be done in a relaxed way. It is a dynamic contraction which indicates, but this contraction begins inside the body and has its objective outside."[33]

A further difference between the work of Stanislavski and that of Grotowski, already mentioned, concerns the "character." In the work of Stanislavski, the "character" is an entirely new being, born from the combination of the character, written by the author, and the actor himself. The actor begins from his "I am" and goes toward the circumstances of the character proposed by the author, arriving at a state of quasi-identification with the character, a new being. Toporkov, in *Stanislavski in Rehearsal*, says: "The creation of a living, *really* living person – this is the goal of high art. The artist who succeeds even once in identifying himself with the stage character he has created is aware that he has accomplished a very great thing and experiences deep happiness."[34]

In the performances of Grotowski, however, the "character" existed more as a public screen which protected the actor. The actor *did not identify* with the "character." One can see this clearly from the case of the Constant Prince of Ryszard Cieslak. The "character" was constructed through the *montage* and was mainly destined for the mind of the spectator; the actor behind this screen maintained his intimacy, his safety. Furthermore, the screen of the "character" kept the mind of the spectator occupied in such a way that the spectator might perceive, with a part of himself more adapted to this task, the hidden process of the actor.

Grotowski told me that the fundamental difference, however, between Stanislavski's "method of physical actions" and his own work, lies in the question of the impulses. Why in Grotowski's work is impulse so important, and why in Stanislavski's work was it not underlined? Because Stanislavski worked on physical actions within the context of the common life of relations: people in "realistic" daily-life circumstances, in some social convention. Grotowski, instead, looks for physical actions in a basic stream of life, not in a social and daily-life situation. And in such a stream of life the impulses are most important. Grotowski affirms that this is the difference between his work and Stanislavski's "method of physical actions."

"REALISTIC" ACTIONS IN EVERYDAY LIFE

The art of the actor is *not* necessarily limited to realistic situations, social games, daily life. Sometimes, the higher the level and the quality of this art, the farther it distances itself from this realistic foundation, entering into realms of exceptionality: the living stream of pure impulses. It is precisely this that has really *always* interested Grotowski in his work with the actor. But to remove the actor's art from the realistic foundation, dear to Stanislavski, and to reach a higher level, it is absolutely necessary to know this foundation.

As a young actor I asked myself: Is all this "realistic work" necessary? I had read for the first time some of the books of Stanislavski, and had found them boring. I was eager to taste the "meat" of acting; I wanted to experience the thrill of emotional revelation. Hopefully, by this point in the text it will be clear, however, that this way of thinking is dilettante. Any true artist will need years of daily practice to arrive at any level in his work. But if it is still not clear why such work is necessary, and how an actor can be helped by a practical understanding of physical actions, let me make an observation of my immediate behavior to see if I can clarify the reason. I remind you that I am now speaking only about realistic situations: daily life and social game.

I am sitting in a café, writing this text. I look out the window concentrating my thoughts. A young woman walks through my field of vision. In that moment I make a sharp expulsion of breath, my spine moves toward the chair back, and I look down toward the page on the table. This sharp breath, the movement of the spine, the looking back to the paper, all happen almost simultaneously (there is also a specific way of inner speaking:

101

"Ah! Thomas, you're working now . . ."). All this is related to a physical action, in some way all this together is a physical action, but it's not yet clear from my description – so far I have spoken mainly of some kind of symptoms. But what is the action?

If someone in the café were observing me attentively in that moment, he would be able to read the logic of my behavior, and see through it, like seeing through a window, some detail of my story. He would have observed: this man upon seeing something outside to which he was drawn, just broke this "drawing" because it was disturbing his work. To cut this "drawing," *what did he do*?

An actor cannot directly "act" this moment as "self-dissatisfaction," because *the will is not able to conduct the emotions*. But he can look down at his papers to begin his work again, shift his spine back to gain more distance from the distraction, with the rhythm of one who decisively cuts from something, and speak inside clearly those thoughts of self-control. In this way, concentrating on the actions (in which the thought is also included), the actor frees his psychological life to react naturally *to what he has done*.

Someone who observes me attentively, can see secrets of my life. He will see something of which maybe even I am not aware. In that moment, if observant, he might know me better than I do. This, supposing that someone in the café is observing me attentively, which may not be the case. But let us suppose instead that this café is a theatre, and that I am an actor. Then hopefully the audience will be present to watch and observe with their senses heightened in the anticipation of receiving something from the performance at hand. Chances are, then, that such details, such actions will be perceived.

Surely spectators have the desire to see something of quality, the desire to have something hidden revealed to them, even unconscious hopes that they might see "something" unknown about themselves. It is the actor's duty to reveal to them this "something," that which was left either unobserved or forgotten. If the actor executes in truth the line of physical actions, he will live genuinely on stage, and this will in its turn be perceived by the spectator.

Physical actions in life flow quickly, often unconsciously. I can understand what happened to me that moment in the café only if I make an attempt to see, to observe and analyze in detail.

102

How can an actor do something in acting if he is not aware of what he is doing in his life? Through inspiration? Inspiration arrives only once, what remains is construction, and this is simply hard work. The actor must first of all *see his own ways of doing* (in daily life) so that he can then *construct* such "doings" (actions) consciously on stage. All this he uses as a springboard to arrive at a genuine experience in which his emotions react naturally – without pumping – to what he is *doing* on stage. The totality of what the actor *does*, with all of its consciously executed details and spontaneous truth, reveals to the spectator something specific about our human condition.

If I go on stage to portray that moment in the café, and I try to act "self-dissatisfaction," I will just sit in the chair and try to pump my psychological life, doing injustice to it. A spectator immediately feels when an actor forces. Even if all your friends tell you after your performance how good you were, both you and your friends know, in a very deep place, the moments in which you forced. You can observe such moments clearly if you observe your own reactions as a spectator. There will arrive a moment when, for example, an actor is trying to achieve falsely an emotional climax. You, as spectator, then start to feel some kind of shame, and for an instant look away, as if a voice in you is saying: "I would rather not see this, I would rather not record this in me." So you avert your eyes to avoid letting that image enter you. Emotional pumping is clearly felt by both spectator and actor instinctively as something unnatural. And it was clear to Stanislavski in the end of his life, and is clear to Grotowski, that emotions are not subject to our will. Don't tamper with them. What we *do*, this is subject to our will.

So, only an actor who can *master what he does* on stage will be able to create a life *on stage*. And in order to master what he does, he must see what is effecting his behavior in daily life. How can an actor do something clearly on stage if he is blind to his own behavior in life? To master his craft, he must investigate others and himself, so that when on stage he can reveal some secret of value that he has remarked in himself and others. These investigations will be like a finger stuck in the wound of the spectator, who will see himself reflected in the mirror of the actor's actions.

How comfortably those in the profession sit when seeing bad theatre! In reality no matter how much we complain, some part of us is content when we see bad theatre. Afterwards, we can speak together comfortably about how bad it was, and when we meet our friends who were in the performance, we can lie just as comfortably about how good it was. The social mask is preserved, nothing moved from its proper place; we go home and sleep soundly, again reassured that the others had no capacity to show us something that we lack, to create in us the shock that one feels when faced with truth.

Stanislavski constructed his methods of work through observation of daily life and social games. We can see this clearly in the book of Nikolai Gorchakov, *Stanislavsky Directs*, in which Stanislavski speaks about how it is possible to understand, while looking through a closed window, a conversation of a couple outside on the street, without even hearing their words; simply by *observing their behavior*.[35]

Grotowski, when working on physical actions, instead did not portray the habitual social game or the realistic details of daily life. In his basic text, *Towards a Poor Theatre*, he says:

"The human being in a moment of shock, of terror, of mortal danger or tremendous joy, doesn't behave 'naturally.' The human being in this type of *inner maximum* makes signs, rhythmically articulates, starts to 'dance,' to 'sing.' Not common gesture or daily 'naturality' but a sign is proper to our primal expression. But in terms of formal technique, it is not a matter of a multiplication of signs, nor of their accumulation (as in oriental theatre where the same signs repeat). In our work, we are seeking *distillation* of signs by eliminating those elements of 'common' behavior which *obscure pure impulses*."[36]

In Grotowski's version, the work on physical actions is only the door for entering into the living stream of impulses, and not a simple reconstruction of daily life. When we analyze "realistic actions," we should see the perspective of the *other level* of this work, which is much more related to *the stream of impulses*. We should also remember that, though investigating our own behavior and the behavior of others in daily life, *we should not form in ourselves an inner observer when we are on stage. In the time of rehearsal or performance, self-observation is a strong adversary* of the actor, and blocks his natural reactions.

104

CONCLUSION ON "REALISTIC" ACTIONS

One day Grotowski said to me: "After the 'System' of Stanislavski, came his 'method of physical actions.' Do you think that Stanislavski would have stopped there? No, he died. *That is why he stopped*. And I simply *continued his research*. That is why some Russians say that 'Grotowski is Stanislavski':[37] that is because I *continued* his research and did *not just repeat* what he had already discovered." In order to continue the investigation of someone else we should know in practice what he already found.

I am asking myself what was the source of Stanislavski's knowledge about little "realistic" actions. Surely it was based on his accurate way of observing daily life. So, sitting once again in the café, I will try, through observation, to push my own understanding of physical actions one step further, as I conclude this text.

A young man is entering the café. He greets the people with a smile, whistling a light melody; the tempo-rhythm of his walk is brisk. He is light on his feet. He sits at a table with his coffee, the newspaper is on the table. His body inclines to look at the front page. But no [. . .] his body now hunches over, sitting with his spine curved in the shape of the letter "C," resting against the back of the chair. His eyes are slightly separating, the left eye drifting more to the left, and the right one drifting more to the right. He sighs. It is as if he no longer sees what is in front of him. He stays in that position without moving for close to twenty seconds. It seems as if he has forgotten about the newspaper, forgotten about the coffee. His forehead now is contracted between the eyebrows. He is no longer smiling. Suddenly he sees again his surroundings. He looks around quickly with small staccato glances to see if someone saw him in the last twenty seconds. Now seeing his coffee, he sips it two times to test if it is hot, and then finishes it in one toss. He puts the cup back in its saucer with an unintentional clack, because he is again looking down, and it seems again he doesn't see what is in front of him. His spine is still in the shape of a "C." He stands slowly. The side of his right index finger now slowly strokes his lips. His hand is now touching his face with one finger entering into his mouth as he moves slowly to the door. His brow is still contracted. He is halfway out the door when he suddenly stops and turns back. He has forgotten to pay for his coffee. He stops touching his face and moves quickly to the counter in a staccato rhythm. His movements while he pays are sharp and sudden. As he leaves the café he is looking down, his lips tightly pressed; his walk is quick, staccato and noisy.

What I described here is *not* the line of physical actions, but the *exterior image* of behavior – and *symptoms* – observed from outside: a moment in the life of this young man. He was not aware of the complexity of what happened to him in these moments. He was not conscious, for example, that he entered the café in one state and left in completely another. We can say that this journey from a "positive" state to a "negative" one was more or less unconscious for him. Probably later on in the day he will at some moment realize he is in a bad mood, but it will be very difficult for him to reconstruct exactly why and how this bad mood started.

Let us suppose, now, that an actor must act this same realistic event. Whereas the young man's behavior was quasi-unconscious, the actor's preparation must be *conscious*, because he must construct the role. The actor, then, must be aware of the little pieces of life with an awareness that others normally do not have. To *do* this reality, the actor must be able to *see it* in its details, then to *construct it*, and then to *live it* on the stage *without self-observation*. He must see that the psychological state of this man was directly related to (and even effected by) his physical behavior; that his original "tempo" of entering the bar was *light* and quick, while his "tempo" of leaving was *heavy* and quick. The actor will know what the precise memory is that he is having as he sits at the table not seeing what is in front of him. The actor will know that there is a direct link between the hunching of the spine while sitting, and the fact that this young man arrived to a negative psychological state. But the actor will

106

not concern himself with the emotional state because he knows he cannot control that with his will. He will concern himself with the way of sitting, with precisely how to keep his body. *Maybe this way of sitting was how that young man sat, for example, the night before when his girlfriend was yelling at him,* accusing him that he did not give her enough. Now he sits in the café the next morning. Until that moment he had forgotten all about the fight from the night before. But now the similar way of sitting calls forth the memory of her red face from the night before. He begins to see her, and hear again the harshness of her voice. He senses again the way her intonations gave him the impulse to hit her (now he sees nothing of the café, hears nothing of what is around him, he is completely absorbed by his memory). He remembers how he just sat faced with her and did nothing. Maybe in this moment his mind speaks: "I did nothing, I did nothing [. . .]" Then the actor must know why he – like the young man – forgets to pay for his coffee: because he leaves the café in the same way he left his girlfriend's house the other night. For him in this moment, the café actually *is* his girlfriend's house. He only sees that, hears her screaming, and escapes . . . forgetting to pay for the coffee. All this must be a clear part of the actor's line of actions; as clear as the temporhythm of his entering (which is different from when he leaves); as clear as the contraction on his forehead as he remembers the lashing quality of his girlfriend's voice, "impossible for listening."

NOTES

1 Cited by Joshua Logan, in Foreword to Sonia Moore, *The Stanislavski System*. New York: Penguin Books, 1984 (1960), p.xvi.
2 Cited by Sonia Moore, *op. cit.*, p.10.
3 Jerzy Grotowski, "Risposta a Stanislavskij" (translation from Polish by Carla Pollastrelli), in *Stanislavskij: L'attore creativo*. Eds Fabrizio Cruciani and Clelia Falletti. Florence: La casa Usher, 1980, p.193 (translation mine).

   The reader should note that Grotowski has reviewed all quotations of his texts and conferences appearing in this volume; in some cases, he has revised them with respect to the translations and current editions.
4 Konstantin S. Stanislavskij, *Il lavoro dell'attore sul personaggio* (*The Work of the Actor on the Role*). Ed. Fausto Malcovati. Roma-Bari, Italy: Editori Laterza, 1988, p.224. I translate all quotations from this book via the Italian edition, based on the final version of the original Russian text, *Rabota aktera nad rol'ju*, revised and corrected by the author.
5 Cited by Vasily O. Toporkov, *Stanislavski in Rehearsal: The Final Years*. Trans. Christine Edwards. New York: Theatre Arts Books, 1979, p.21.
6 Jerzy Grotowski, *Towards a Poor Theatre*. Holstebro: Odin Teatrets Forlag, 1968.
7 Reported by Vasily O. Toporkov, *op. cit.*, p.160.
8 Sonia Moore, *op. cit.*, p.23 (italics mine).
9 Jerzy Grotowski, "Le Prince constant de Ryszard Cieslak: Rencontre *Hommage à Ryszard Cieslak*, 9 décembre 1990." Organized by the Académie Expérimentale des Théâtres in collaboration with Théâtre de l'Europe. In *Ryszard Cieslak, acteur-emblème des années soixante*. Ouvrage collectif sous la direction de Georges Banu. Paris: Actes Sud-Papiers, 1992, pp.13–19.
10 Vasily O. Toporkov, *op. cit.*
11 Jerzy Grotowski, conference at Liège, Cirque Divers, 2 January 1986. Unpublished transcription of a tape recording, in French, consulted through Grotowski (translation mine).
12 Jerzy Grotowski, "Tu es le fils de quelqu'un" in *Europe* n.726,

October 1989. Paris: Europe et Messidor, pp.21–24. I translate from the French version of this text, the one most recently revised by the author.

13 Jerzy Grotowski, "Tu es le fils de quelqu'un," pp.16–17.

14 Jerzy Grotowski, conference at Santarcangelo, Italy, 18 July 1988. Unpublished transcription of a tape recording, in French, consulted through Grotowski (translation mine).

15 Reported by Vasily O. Toporkov, *op. cit.*, p.173.

16 Cited by Sonia Moore, *The Stanislavski System*. New York: Penguin Books, 1979 (1960), p.23.

17 Jerzy Grotowski, "C'était une sorte de volcan," interview in *Les dossiers H.* Trans. Magda Zlotowska. Paris: Editions l'Age d'Homme et Bruno de Panafieu, 1992, p.102.

18 Reported by Vasily O. Toporkov, *op. cit.*, p.160.

19 Jerzy Grotowski, conference at Santarcangelo.

20 *Ibid.*

21 *Ibid.*

22 Jerzy Grotowski, conference at Liège.

23 *Ibid.*

24 Jerzy Grotowski, "Performer" in *Centro di Lavoro di Jerzy Grotowski*. Pontedera, Italy: Centro per la Sperimentazione e la Ricerca Teatrale, 1988, pp.39–40.

25 Jerzy Grotowski, conference at Santarcangelo.

26 *Ibid.*

27 Peter Brook, "Grotowski, Art as a Vehicle" in *Centro di Lavoro di Jerzy Grotowski*. Pontedera, Italy: Centro per la Sperimentazione e la Ricerca Teatrale, 1988, pp.34–35 (italics mine).

28 Jerzy Grotowski, "C'était une sorte de volcan," *op. cit.*, p.102.

29 Konstantin S. Stanislavskij, *op. cit.*, p.217.

30 Jerzy Grotowski, "C'était une sorte de volcan," *op. cit.*, p.99.

31 Jerzy Grotowski, conference at Liège.

32 *Ibid.*

33 *Ibid.*

34 Vasily O. Toporkov, *op. cit.*, p.218.

35 Nikolai Gorchakov, *Stanislavsky Directs*. New York: Limelight Editions, 1985 (1954), pp.314–316.

36 Jerzy Grotowski, *Towards a Poor Theatre*, *op. cit.*, pp.17–18.

37 For example, Anatolij Vassiliev in his text, "Dopoki Grotowski . . ." in *Notatnik Teatralny* (Spring 1991, Wroclaw, Poland, p.10), says: "When I studied directing [in a Moscow theatre institute] and in the corridors floated this name, Grotowski, for me it was Stanislavski."

QUOTED TEXTS

Brook, Peter. "Grotowski, Art as a Vehicle." In *Centro di Lavoro di Jerzy Grotowski*. Pontedera, Italy: Centro per la Sperimentazione e la Ricerca Teatrale, 1988.

Gorchakov, Nikolai M. *Stanislavsky Directs*. New York: Limelight Editions, 1985 (1954).

Grotowski, Jerzy. *Towards a Poor Theatre*. Holstebro: Odin Teatrets Forlag, 1968.

Grotowski, Jerzy. "Risposta a Stanislavskij." Trans. Carla Pollastrelli. In *Stanislavskij: L'attore creativo*. Eds Fabrizio Cruciani and Clelia Falletti. Florence: La casa Usher, 1980.

Grotowski, Jerzy. Unpublished conference. Liège: Cirque Divers, 2 January 1986.

Grotowski, Jerzy. "Performer." In *Centro di Lavoro di Jerzy Grotowski*. Pontedera, Italy: Centro per la Sperimentazione e la Ricerca Teatrale, 1988.

Grotowski, Jerzy. Unpublished conference. Santarcangelo, Italy, 18 July 1988.

Grotowski, Jerzy. "Tu es le fils de quelqu'un." In *Europe* n.726, October 1989. Paris: Europe et Messidor.

Grotowski, Jerzy. "C'était une sorte de volcan." In *Les dossiers H*. Paris: Editions l'Age d'Homme et Bruno de Panafieu, 1992.

Grotowski, Jerzy. "Le Prince constant de Ryszard Cieslak: Rencontre *Hommage à Ryszard Cieslak*, 9 décembre 1990." Organized by Académie Expérimentale des Théâtres in collaboration with Théâtre de l'Europe. In *Ryszard Cieslak, acteur-emblème des années soixante*. Ouvrage collectif sous la direction de Georges Banu. Paris: Actes Sud-Papiers, 1992.

Moore, Sonia. *The Stanislavski System*. New York: Penguin Books, 1979, 1984 (1960).

Stanislavskij, Konstantin S. *Il lavoro dell'attore sul personaggio*. Ed. Fausto Malcovati. Roma-Bari, Italy: Editori Laterza, 1988.

Toporkov, Vasily O. *Stanislavski in Rehearsal: The Final Years*. Trans. Christine Edwards. New York: Theatre Arts Books, 1979.

Vassiliev, Anatolij. "Dopoki Grotowski. . . " In *Notatnik Teatralny*, Spring 1991. Wroclaw, Poland.

111

FROM THE THEATRE COMPANY TO ART AS VEHICLE

by Jerzy Grotowski

The present text is based on transcriptions of two of Jerzy Grotowski's conferences: October 1989 in Modena, Italy and May 1990 at the University of California, Irvine.

On the basis of the Italian version translated by Carla Pollastrelli, the English translation of this text is by Thomas Richards, Michel A. Moos, and the author.

Jerzy Grotowski has extensively revised the English text which (as well as the French version) should presently be considered the final redaction of "From the Theatre Company to Art as Vehicle."

FROM THE THEATRE COMPANY TO ART AS VEHICLE

Jerzy Grotowski

I

When I speak of "theatre company," I mean the theatre of ensemble, the long-term work of a group. Work which is not linked in any particular way to the concepts of the avant-garde and which constitutes the basis for professional theatre of our century, the beginnings of which go back to the end of the 1800s. But we can also say that it was Stanislavski who developed this modern notion of the theatre company as foundation for professional work. I think to begin with Stanislavski is correct, because, whatever our aesthetic orientation in the field of theatre may be, we in some way understand who Stanislavski was. He did not busy himself with experimental theatre or the avant-garde; he conducted a solid and systematic work on craft.

But what was before the theatre of ensemble? We can imagine in the nineteenth century, above all in Central and Eastern Europe, certain families of actors in which, for example, the father and the mother were actors, and the old uncle was the director: even though in reality his function was just to indicate to the actors "you enter through this door and sit in that chair," he would also take care of the garments and props when necessary. The grandson was an actor as well and, when he married, his wife became an actress; later on if a friend arrived, even he joined the theatre family.

These families had very short rehearsal periods, more or less five days to prepare for an opening. So the actors of that time had developed a prodigious memory: they learned a text with great speed and in a few days were able to speak it by heart. But since they would sometimes get confused, a prompter was necessary.

If I look at this period from a distance, I think that the work of those people was not so bad. They were not able to elaborate all the details of their performance, but they knew that the details had to be there. Besides, they understood the dramatic situations which had to appear, and above all, they knew that they had to find a way of being alive through their behavior. From this point of view, I believe that what they did was much better than rehearsing for four or five weeks, because four or five weeks is too little to prepare the true score of a role and too much to try to catch the life just by improvising.

What is the proper length of time for rehearsals?

It depends. Stanislavski often rehearsed for one year and it even happened to him to work on the same play for three years. Brecht also rehearsed for long periods. But there does exist something like a medium duration. During the 1960s in Poland, for example, the normal period of rehearsal was three months. For young directors who are preparing their first or second performance, it can be advantageous to have before them a set date for the opening, using a relatively brief period to rehearse, for example, two and a half months. Otherwise they can indulge themselves in a waste of time: in the initial stage of their craft, they are full of material gathered in the course of life, material which has not yet been channeled into the performances.

On the other hand, certain directors, apparently experienced, admit that toward the end of the established period of four weeks they don't know anymore what to do. Here is the problem: a lack of knowledge about what the work with the actor and the work on the mise-en-scène is. If you want to obtain in one month the same results that earlier the families of actors obtained in five days, it's logical that very quickly you won't know anymore what to work on. The rehearsals become more and more of a summary. What is the cause? Commercialization. The theatre companies are disappearing, giving way to the *industry* of performance; above all in the United States, but also increasingly in Europe. The theatres are becoming agencies that hire out the director who in turn – alone or with the casting director – selects, from tens or hundreds of candidates, the actors for the programed premiere; then begin the rehearsals which last some weeks. What does all this mean?

It's like cutting the forest without planting the trees. The actors

116

don't have the possibility to find something which is a discovery, both artistic and personal. They can't. In order to cope, they have to exploit that which they already know how to do and which has given them success – and this goes against creativity. Because creativity is rather to discover that which you don't know. This is the key reason why companies are needed. They provide the possibility of renewing artistic discoveries. In the work of a theatre group, a specific continuity is necessary: through each of the successive plays, over a long period of time, with the possibility for an actor to pass from one type of role to another. The actors should have time for research. So it is not to cut the forest, but to plant the seeds of creativity. This started with Stanislavski.

According to "natural laws," the creative life of a company doesn't last too long. Ten to fourteen years, no more. Then the company dries up, unless it reorganizes and introduces new forces; otherwise it dies. We should not see the theatre company as an end in itself. If the company transforms into merely a secure place, it arrives at a state of inertia; then it is no longer important, whether there are artistic victories or not. Everything arranges itself as in a bureaucratic enterprise – which drags on, drags on as if time stops. Here is the danger.

II

In the United States there exist numerous university drama departments and some are fairly large. Many professors work in the name of Stanislavski, looking for, in their own measure, that which Stanislavski indicated, or claiming to develop that which Stanislavski proposed. And here we are faced with an absurdity. How is it possible to study Stanislavski for two or three years and prepare an opening in four weeks (as is often done in these departments)? Stanislavski would never have accepted it. For him, the minimum period of work on a performance was several months, and the opening took place only when the actors were ready.

Outside of the drama departments an explanation exists: the lack of funds. But inside these departments usually there are funds, even if minimal and – what's more – there is time. They can work for four, five, nine months, because they have time. Drama departments take as actors their students (who are not paid), so the rehearsals can be as long as needed; but generally they are not.

In drama departments, therefore, the possibility exists (within the frame of the program of studies) to create something that could function like a theatre group – and not for a political or philosophical principle, but for professional reasons: not to lose time with every new piece with the pretense of making great discoveries, but simply, to look for what the possibilities are, and how one can go beyond them. Upon finishing a piece, you should be prepared for starting the next one.

In 1964, at my Teatr Laboratorium in Poland, we made a performance based on *Hamlet*, then considered a disaster by the critics. For me it wasn't a disaster. For me it was the preparation of a very special work and, in effect, several years later I did *Apocalypsis cum figuris*. To draw nearer in this special approach, it was necessary to work with the same persons, the same company. The first step (*Hamlet*) proved incomplete. It didn't miss the mark, but it wasn't fulfilled right to the end. Yet it was close to the discovery of some essential possibilities. Then, with the other performance, it was possible to take the next step. There are many elements related to craft that need long term work. And this is possible only if the company exists.

If one works in the name of Stanislavski, one should begin with the minimum that he requested: the time for the rehearsals, the elaboration of the acting score, and the work in a group. Otherwise, return to the families of actors and do the performance in five days. This is perhaps better than a miserable four weeks.

III

I will now pass to the following theme. In the performing arts, there exists a chain with many different links. In the theatre we have a visible link – the performance – and another, almost invisible: the rehearsals. Rehearsals are not only a preparation for the opening, they are for the actor a terrain of discoveries, about himself, his possibilities, his chances to transcend his limits. Rehearsals are a great adventure if we work seriously. Let's take Toporkov's important book on the work of Stanislavski, entitled *Stanislavski in Rehearsal*. Here we see that the most interesting things happened during the rehearsals of

Tartuffe, when Stanislavski was not even thinking of making a public performance. For him, the work on *Tartuffe* was an internal work for the actors, whom he treated like the future masters of acting, or as the future directors, and he showed them in what consists the adventure of rehearsals.

Fleming was not searching for penicillin; he and his colleagues were looking for something else. But his research was systematic, and then – there it is – penicillin appeared. One can say something similar regarding rehearsals. We are looking for something of which we have only a preliminary notion, some concept. If we search intensely and thoroughly, maybe we don't find that at all, but something else can appear which can give a different direction to the whole work. I remember the situation when the Teatr Laboratorium began to work on *Samuel Zborowski* of Slowacki, and, without realizing it, we changed direction during the rehearsals. After a few months, in fact, some elements appeared – they were alive and interesting, but they didn't have anything to do with the text of *Samuel Zborowski*. As director, I was on the side of that which was truly alive. I didn't look for a way to insert it into the structure of the projected performance; instead I observed what would happen if we developed it. After some time we became more precise, and this brought us to the text of *The Grand Inquisitor* of Dostoevski. In the end *Apocalypsis cum figuris* appeared. It appeared in the middle of rehearsals on another performance; I would say it appeared in the seed of the rehearsals.

So, rehearsals are something very special. Here, the sole spectator is present – he whom I call "the director as professional spectator." Thus we have: rehearsals for the performance and rehearsals not entirely for the performance, much more to discover the possibilities of the actors. In reality, we have already spoken about three links of a very long chain: the link of performance, the link of rehearsals for the performance, the link of rehearsals not quite for the performance ... This, at one extremity of the chain. At the other extremity, we find something very ancient but unknown in our culture of today: Art as vehicle – the term that Peter Brook has used to define my present work. Normally in theatre (that is to say, in theatre of performance, in Art as presentation), one works on the vision that should appear in the perception of the spectator. If all of the elements of the performance are elaborated and correctly assembled (the montage), an effect appears in the perception of the spectator, a vision, a certain story; to some degree the performance appears not on the stage but in the perception of the spectator. This is the nature of Art as presentation. At the other extremity of the long chain of the performing arts is Art as vehicle, which looks to create the montage *not* in the perception of the spectators, but *in the artists who do*. This has already existed in the past, in the ancient Mysteries.

IV

In my life I passed through different phases of work. In the theatre of performances (Art as presentation) – which I consider a very important phase, an extraordinary adventure with long-term effects – I arrived at a point in which I was no longer interested in doing new performances.

So I suspended my work as constructor of performances and continued, concentrating on discovering the prolongation of the chain: the links *after* those of performance and rehearsing; thus emerged paratheatre, that is to say, participatory theatre (meaning, with the *active* participation of people from the outside). Herein was the *Holiday – the day that is holy*: human, but almost sacred, consisting in a "disarming of oneself" – reciprocal and total. What were the conclusions? In the first years, when a small group worked thoroughly on this for months and months, and was later joined only by a few new participants from the outside, things happened which were on the border of a miracle. However afterwards, when, in light of this experience, we made other versions, with a view to including more participants – or when the base group had not passed first through a long period of intrepid work – certain fragments functioned well, but the whole descended to some extent into an emotive soup between the people, or rather into a kind of animation. From paratheatre was born (as the link *after*) Theatre of Sources, which dealt with the source of different traditional techniques, with "what precedes the differences." In this research, the approach was rather solitary. Often working outdoors, we were looking mainly for what the human being can do with his own solitude, how it can be transformed into force and a deep relationship with what is called the natural environment. "The senses and their objects," "the circulation of attention," "the Current 'glimpsed' by one

120

while he is in movement," "the living body in the living world" – all this in some way became the countersign of this work. With Theatre of Sources we arrived at strong and very alive processes even if, in some respect, we did not transcend the stages of searching tentatively: there was not enough time to continue as the program was cut (I had to leave Poland).

Both paratheatre and Theatre of Sources can entail a limitation – that of fixation on the "horizontal" plane (with its vital forces, prevalently corporeal and instinctive) instead of simply taking off from it, as from a runway. Although this is avoidable if one pays great attention, it's right to mention it, because the predominance of the vital element can block on the horizontal plane: this does not allow one to pass in action *above* this plane.

The present work, which I consider for me as final, as the point of arrival, is Art as vehicle. On the way, I have made a long trajectory – from Art as presentation to Art as vehicle (which, on the other hand, is linked to my most old interests). Paratheatre and Theatre of Sources were on the line of this trajectory.

Paratheatre made it possible to put to the test the very essence of determination: to not hide oneself in anything.

Theatre of Sources revealed real possibilities. But it was clear that we could not realize them *in toto* if we did not pass beyond a somewhat "impromptu" level. I never broke with the thirst that motivated Theatre of Sources. Nevertheless, Art as vehicle is not oriented along the same axis – the work is trying to go consciously and deliberately above the horizontal plane with its vital forces, and this way through has become the main issue: "verticality." On the other hand, Art as vehicle is concentrated on rigor, on details, on precision – comparable to that of the performances of the Teatr Laboratorium. But attention! It's not a return toward Art as presentation; it is *the other extremity of the same chain.*

V

From this point of view, I will make some specifications about the work at my Workcenter in Pontedera, Italy.

One pole of work in the Workcenter is dedicated to formation (in the sense of permanent education), in the field of song, of text, of physical actions (analogous to those of Stanislavski), of the "plastic" and "physical" exercises for actors.

The other pole encompasses that which proceeds toward Art as vehicle. The rest of this text deals with this research, because it is something unknown or, in a sense, forgotten in the contemporary world.

We can say "Art as vehicle," but also "objectivity of ritual" or "Ritual arts." When I speak of ritual, I am referring neither to a ceremony nor a celebration, and even less to an improvisation with the participation of people from the outside. Nor do I speak of a synthesis of different ritual forms coming from different places. When I refer to ritual, I speak of its objectivity; this means that the elements of the Action are the instruments to work *on the body, the heart and the head of the doers.*

In Art as vehicle, from the point of view of technical elements, everything is almost like in the performing arts; we work on song, on impulses, on forms of movement, even textual motifs appear. And all is reduced to the strictly necessary, until a structure appears, a structure as precise and worked out as in a performance: the *Action*.

Now someone might ask: What, then, is the difference between this objectivity of ritual and a performance? Is the difference only in the fact that the public is not invited?

This question is legitimate; I want, therefore, to indicate some premises which clarify the difference between Art as presentation (a performance) and Art as vehicle.

One difference, among others, is in the seat of the montage.

In a performance, the seat of the montage is in the perception of the spectator; in Art as vehicle, the seat of the montage is in the *doers*, in the artists who do.

I want to give you an example of the seat of the montage *in the perception of the spectator*. Let us take the Constant Prince of Ryszard Cieslak in the Teatr Laboratorium. Before meeting in work on the role with his partners in the performance, for months and months Cieslak worked alone with me. Nothing in his work was linked to the martyr that, in the drama of Calderon/Slowacki, is the theme of the role of the Constant Prince. All the river of life in the actor was linked to a certain memory, which was very far from any darkness, any suffering. His long monologues were linked to the actions which belonged to that concrete memory from his life, to the most minute actions and physical and vocal impulses of that remembered moment. It was a relatively short moment from his life – we can say some

122

tens of minutes, a time of love from his early youth. This referred to that kind of love which, as it can only arrive in adolescence, carries all its sensuality, all that which is carnal, but, at the same time, behind that, something totally different that is not carnal, or which is carnal in another way, and which is much more like a prayer. It's as if, between these two sides, appears a bridge which is a *carnal prayer*. The moment of which I speak was, therefore, immune from every dark connotation, it was as if this remembered adolescent liberated himself with his body from the body itself, as if he liberated himself – step after step – from the heaviness of the body, from any painful aspect. And, on the river of the memory, of its most minute impulses and actions, he put the monologues of the Constant Prince.

Yes, the cycle of the actor's personal associations can be one thing, and the line that appears in the perception of the spectator another thing. But between these two different things there must exist a genuine relation, a single deep root, even if it is well hidden. Otherwise everything becomes whatever, just casual. In the case of the work with Ryszard Cieslak on the Constant Prince, this root was linked to our reading – before we even started to work – of the *Spiritual Canticle* by John of the Cross (which rejoins the biblical tradition of the *Song of Songs*). In this hidden reference, the relation between the soul and the True – or, if you want, between Man and God – is the relationship of the Bride with her Beloved. It is this that led Cieslak toward his memory of an experience of love so unique that it became a carnal prayer.

But the content of the play by Calderon/Slowacki, the logic of the text, the structure of the performance around and in relation to him, the narrative elements and the characters of the drama, all this suggested he was a prisoner, a martyr whom they try to crush and who refuses to submit to laws which he does not accept. And through this agony of the martyr, he arrives at the peak.

This was the story for the spectator, but not for the actor. His partners around him, dressed as prosecutors of a military tribunal, provoked an association with the contemporary history of Poland. But this specific allusion was not the key. The foundation of the montage was the narration (around the actor who played the Constant Prince) which created the story of a martyr: the mise-en-scène, the structure of the written text and, most importantly, the actions of the other actors who, for their part, had their own motivations. No one sought to play, for example, a military prosecutor; everyone played in connection with the matters of his own life, strictly structured and put into the form of that story "according to Calderon/Slowacki."

So, where did the performance appear?

In a certain sense this *totality* (the montage) appeared not on the stage, but in the perception of the *spectator*. The seat of the montage was the perception of the spectator. That which the spectator caught was the intended montage, while that which the actors did – that's another story.

To make the montage in the spectator's perception is not the duty of the actor, but of the director. The actor should rather seek to *liberate* himself from the dependence on the spectator, if he doesn't want to lose the very seed of creativity. To make the montage in the spectator's perception is the task of the director, and it is one of the most important elements of his craft. As director of *The Constant Prince*, I worked with premeditation to create this type of montage, and so that the majority of the spectators captured the *same* montage: the story of a martyr, of a prisoner surrounded by his persecutors, who look to crush him, but in the same time are fascinated by him, etc. ... All this was conceived in a quasi-mathematical way, so that this montage functioned and was accomplishing itself in the perception of the spectator.

On the contrary, when I speak of Art as vehicle, I refer to a montage whose seat is *not in the perception of the spectator but in the doers*. It is not that the doers agree between themselves about what the common montage will be, it is not that they share some common definition about what they will do. No, not verbal agreement, no spoken definition: It is necessary, through the very actions themselves to discover how to approach – step by step – toward the essential. In this case the seat of the montage is in the doers.

We can also use another language: the elevator. The performance is like a big elevator of which the actor is the operator. The spectators are in this elevator, the performance transports them from one form of event to another. If this elevator functions for the spectators, it means that the montage is well done.

Art as vehicle is like a very primitive elevator: it's some kind of basket pulled by a cord, with which the doer lifts himself toward a more subtle energy, to descend *with this* to the instinctual body. This is the *objectivity* of the ritual. If Art as vehicle functions, this objectivity exists and the basket moves for those who do the *Action*.

Various elements of work are similar in all the performing arts, but precisely in this difference between the elevators (one is the elevator for the spectators, and the other, the primordial one, for the doers) – as well as in the difference between the montage in the perception of the spectators and the montage in the artists who do – lies the distinction between Art as presentation and Art as vehicle.

In Art as vehicle the impact on the doer is the result. But this result is not the content; the content is in the passage from the heavy to the subtle.

When I speak of the image of the primordial elevator, and therefore of Art as vehicle, I refer to verticality. Verticality – we can see this phenomenon in categories of energy: heavy but organic energies (linked to the forces of life, to instincts, to sensuality) and other energies, more subtle. The question of verticality means to pass from a so-called coarse level – in a certain sense, one could say an "everyday level" – to a level of energy more subtle or even toward the *higher connection*. At this point to say more about it wouldn't be right. I simply indicate the passage, the direction. There, there is another passage as well: if one approaches the higher connection – that means, if we are speaking in terms of energy, if one approaches the much more subtle energy – then there is also the question of descending, while at the same time bringing this subtle something into the more common reality, which is linked to the "density" of the body.

The point is not to renounce part of our nature – all should retain its natural place: the body, the heart, the head, something that is "under our feet" and something that is "over the head." All like a vertical line, and this verticality should be held taut between organicity and *the awareness*. *Awareness* means the consciousness which is not linked to language (the machine for thinking), but to Presence.

One can compare all this to Jacob's ladder. The Bible speaks of the story of Jacob who fell asleep with his head on a stone and had a vision; he saw, upright upon the earth, a great ladder, and perceived the forces or – if you prefer – the angels, who ascended and descended.

125

Yes, it's very important to make, in Art as vehicle, a Jacob's ladder; but for this ladder to function, every rung must be well made. Otherwise the ladder will break; all depends on the artisanal competence with which one works, on the quality of the details, on the quality of the actions and the rhythm, on the order of the elements; all should be impeccable from the point of view of craft. Instead, usually if someone looks in art for his Jacob's ladder, he imagines that it depends simply on good will; so he looks for something amorphous, a kind of soup, and he dissolves himself in his own illusions. I repeat: the ladder of Jacob should be constructed with artisanal credibility.

VI

The ritual songs of the ancient tradition give a support in the construction of the rungs of that vertical ladder. It is not a question only of capturing the melody with its precision, even if without this nothing is possible. It is also necessary to find a tempo-rhythm with all of its fluctuations *inside* the melody. But above all, it is a question of something that constitutes the proper sonority: vibratory qualities which are so tangible that in a certain way they become the meaning of the song. In other words, the song becomes the meaning itself through the vibratory qualities; even if one doesn't understand the words, reception alone of the vibratory qualities is enough. When I speak of this "meaning," I speak at the same time of the impulses of the body; that is, the sonority and the impulses *are* the meaning, directly. To discover the vibratory qualities of a ritual song of an ancient tradition, it is necessary to discover the difference between the melody and the vibratory qualities. This is very important in societies in which oral transmission has disappeared. For this reason it is important for us. In our world, in our culture one understands, for example, the melody as a succession of notes, a notation of notes. This is the melody. It is not possible to discover the vibratory qualities of the song if one begins, let's say, to improvise; I don't mean that one sings out of tune, but, if one sings the same song five times and each time a different one appears, it means that the melody has not been fixed. The melody should be totally dominated, in order that one can develop the work on the vibratory qualities. But, even if it is absolutely necessary to be precise in the melody in order to dis-

126

cover the vibratory qualities, the melody is not the same as the vibratory qualities. It is a delicate point, because – to use a metaphor – it's as if the modern man doesn't hear the difference between the sound of a piano and the sound of a violin. The two types of resonance are very different; but the modern man looks just for the melodic line, without catching differences of resonance.

The song of tradition is like a person. When people begin to work on a supposed ritual, on account of a coarseness of ideas and associations, they begin to look for a state of possession or presumed trance, which reduces itself to chaos and improvisations in which one does anything whatever. Forget all these exoticisms! What is needed is just to see that the traditional song, with the impulses linked to it, is "a person." And so: How to discover this? Only in practice; but I can give you an image, so that you know what I am speaking of. There exist ancient songs in which one easily discovers that they are women, and there are other songs, which are masculine; there are songs in which it's easy to discover that they are adolescents or even children – it's a song-child; and others that are old men – it's a song-old man. Then one can ask: this song, is it a woman or a man? Is it a child, an adolescent, an old man? – the number of possibilities is enormous. But to ask oneself this type of question *is not the method*. If one transforms it into a method, it becomes *flat and stupid*. And yet: a song of tradition is a living being, yes, not every song is a human being, there is also the song-animal, there is the song-force.

When we begin to catch the vibratory qualities, this finds its rooting in the impulses and the actions. And then, all of a sudden, that song begins to *sing us*. That ancient song sings me; I don't know anymore if I am finding that song or if I am that song. Beware! This is the moment in which vigilance is necessary, not to become the property of the song – yes, *keep standing*.

The traditional song, insofar as it is an instrument of verticality, is comparable to mantra in the Hindu or Buddhist culture. The mantra is a sonic form, very elaborated, which englobes the position of the body and the breathing, and which makes appear a determined vibration in a tempo-rhythm so precise that it influences the tempo-rhythm of the mind. The mantra is a short incantation, effective like an instrument; it doesn't serve the spectators, but those who practice it. The songs of tradition also serve those who practice them. Each of these songs, which were formed in a long arc of time and were utilized for sacred or ritual purposes (I would say that they were used as an element of vehicle), brings different types of results. For example, one result is stimulating, another brings calm (this example is simplistic and crude; not only because there are a great many possibilities, but above all because among these possibilities there are those which touch a much more subtle domain).

Why do I speak of mantra and then move toward the song of tradition? Because in the work which interests me, mantra is less applicable, given that the mantra is far from the organic approach. On the contrary, the traditional songs (like those of the Afro-Caribbean line) are rooted in organicity. It's always the song-body, it's never the song dissociated from the impulses of life that run through the body; in the song of tradition, it is no longer a question of the position of the body or the manipulation of the breath, but of the impulses and the little actions. Because the impulses which run in the body are exactly that which carries the song.

There exist differences of impact between the single songs of tradition. From the point of view of verticality toward the subtle and the descent of the subtle to a level of reality more ordinary, there exists the necessity of a "logical" structure: a specific song cannot locate itself either a little before or a little after in respect to the other songs – its place must be evident. On the other hand: I would say that after a hymn of a highly subtle quality, if – for example – continuing the line of the *Action*, we need to descend to the level of another more instinctual song, we should not simply lose this hymn, but maintain a trace of its quality *inside* ourself.

What I have said so far simply touches on some examples of the work on the songs of tradition. Moreover, the rungs of this vertical ladder, which must be elaborated in solid craftsmanship, are not only the songs of tradition and the way in which we work on them, but also the text as living word, the forms of movement, the *logic* of the smallest actions (the fundamental thing, it seems to me, is always to precede the form by what should precede it, by a process which leads to the form). Each of these aspects can require, indeed, a separate chapter.

I would like, however, to make some observations related to

the work on the body. One can resolve the question of the obedience of the body through two different approaches; I don't wish to say that a complex or double approach is impossible, but, to be clear, I prefer to limit myself here to two distinct approaches.

The first approach is to put the body into a state of obedience by taming it. It is possible to compare this approach with the classical "balletic treatment" of the body, or that of certain types of athletics. The danger of this approach is that the body develops itself as muscular entity, therefore not sufficiently flexible and "empty" to be a pervious channel for the energies. The other danger – even greater – is that one strengthens the separation between the head which directs and the body, which becomes like a manipulated marionette. In spite of this, I should underline that the dangers and the limits of this approach can be overcome, if one is fully conscious of these limits and dangers, and if the instructor is perspicacious – one often finds examples in work on the body in the martial arts.

The second approach is to challenge the body. To challenge it by giving it tasks, objectives that seem to exceed the capacities of the body. It's a question of inviting the body to the "impossible" and making it discover that the "impossible" can be divided into small pieces, small elements, and made possible. In this second approach, the body becomes obedient without knowing that it should be obedient. It becomes a channel open to the energies, and finds the conjunction between the rigor of elements and the flow of life ("spontaneity"). Thus the body does not feel like a tamed or domestic animal, but rather like an animal wild and proud. The gazelle pursued by a tiger runs with a lightness, a harmony of movement that is incredible. If one watches this in slow motion in a documentary, this run of gazelle and tiger gives an image of life which is full and paradoxically joyous. The two approaches are entirely legitimate. In my creative life, however, I have always been more interested by the *second* approach.

VII

If one looks for Art as vehicle, the necessity of arriving at a structure which can be repeated – to arrive, so to say, at the *opus* – is even greater than in the work on a performance destined for the public. One cannot work on oneself (to use the term of Stanislavski), if one is not inside something which is structured and can be repeated, which has a beginning a middle and an end, something in which every element has its logical place, technically necessary. *All this determined from the point of view of that verticality toward the subtle and of its (the subtle) descent toward the density of the body*. The structure elaborated in details – the *Action* – is the key; if the structure is missing, all dissolves.

So, we work on our opus: the *Action*. The work takes at least eight hours a day (often much more), six days a week, and lasts for years in a systematic way; it includes the songs, the score of reactions, archaic models of movement, the word, so ancient that it's almost always anonymous. And in this way we build something concrete, a structure comparable to that of a performance, which, however, does not try to create the montage in the perception of the spectators, but in the artists who do it.

In the construction of the *Action*, the majority of the source-elements come from (in one way or another) the Occidental tradition. They are linked to that which I call "the cradle," in this case: the cradle of the Occident. Speaking by approximation, without pretense of scientific precision, the cradle of the Occident included Ancient Egypt, the land of Israel, Greece, and Ancient Syria. There exist, for example, textual elements of which the origin cannot be determined, save for the fact of their transmission through Egypt, but there also exists a version in Greek. The initiatic songs which we use (both those of Black Africa and those of the Caribbean) are rooted in the African tradition; we approach them in the work as a reference to something living in Ancient Egypt (or in its roots), we approach them as belonging to the cradle.

But here we find another problem: we cannot really understand our own tradition (at least in my case) without comparing it with a different cradle. It's that which we can call corroboration. In the perspective of corroboration, the Oriental cradle is for me very important. Not only for technical reasons (the techniques there were highly elaborated), but for personal reasons. Because precisely the sources of the Oriental cradle had a direct impact on me when I was a child and adolescent, long before I did theatre. Corroboration often opens unexpected perspectives and breaks mental habits. For example, in the Oriental tradition, that which we call the Absolute can be approached as the Mother. Instead, in Europe, the accent is placed more on the Father. It's only one example, but it sheds an unexpected light also on the words of our distant predecessors in the Occident. Technical corroboration is palpable: one sees the analogies and the differences; an example of this was given when I analyzed both the functioning of the mantra and the traditional song.

What I want to remind you of is that, in the work on Art as vehicle at the Workcenter in Pontedera, when we construct the opus – the *Action* – our sources refer mainly to the Occidental cradle.

The *Action*: the performative structure objectified in details. This work is not destined for spectators; however, from time to time, the presence of witnesses can be needed. On one hand, so that the quality of the work is tested and, on the other, so that it's not a purely private matter, useless to others. Who have been our witnesses? At first they were specialists and artists individually invited. But later, we invited companies of "young theatre" and theatre of research. They were not spectators (because the performative structure – the *Action* – was not created aiming at them), but somehow they were *like* spectators. When a theatre group visited us, or if our people visited a theatre group, each would observe both the created works and the exercises of the other (however: no reciprocal active participation, for we are not doing participatory theatre).

In this way, over the last few years, we have met with almost sixty theatre groups. These meetings were not organized by means of the press or by written request. The meetings were protected from any kind of publicity, and only the visiting group and the hosting group took part, without any other external witness. Thanks to these precautions, what we had to say to one another after the meeting of work was sufficiently free from the fear of being criticized, or being put under a deceptive light. It's important that it's not a matter of groups arriving by means of an announcement. No group which presented itself on its own, only those which we found through our own means; no bureaucracy, no mechanicity in the way in which we came to find an invited company. It's by this informal and discreet way that it was possible for us also to find small groups with no money, without publicity, but who are really looking to understand what functions and what doesn't function in their work; to understand not theoretically, not in the order

131

of ideas, but through simple, artisanal examples linked to craft.

This is just an example of how Art as vehicle, more or less isolated, can still maintain an alive relation in the field of theatre, through the unique presence of colleagues of the profession. We never look to change the objectives of others. It would not be correct, because their efforts are connected, in a certain manner, with other categories of meaning, circumstances of work, notions about art.

VIII

Can one work on two registers in the same performative structure? On Art as presentation (the making of the public performance) and, at the same time, on Art as vehicle?

This is the question that I ask myself. Theoretically, I see that it should be possible; in my practice I have done these two things in different periods of my life: Art as presentation and Art as vehicle. But are they both possible within the same performative structure? If one works on Art as vehicle, but wants to use this as something spectacular, the emphasis easily shifts and, therefore, in addition to every other difficulty, the sense of all this risks to become equivocal. So we could say that it's a very difficult question to resolve. But if I truly had faith in the fact that, in spite of everything, it could be resolved, surely I would be tempted to do it, I admit.

It is evident that, if in the course of our work on Art as vehicle, we have met with almost sixty groups – sixty companies of "young theatre" and theatre of research – there might have appeared a certain influence so delicate that it's *practically anonymous*, at the level of technical details, of details of craft – regarding precision, for example – and this is legitimate. But in some of these groups I remark that, from the fact itself of having seen our work on Art as vehicle, they grasp in some way what it is and ask themselves how to approach something similar in their own work, which is nevertheless destined for the making of performances. If this question is posed on a mental level, formulated, methodologic, etc., then I tell them that they should not follow us in this field, that they should not look for Art as vehicle in their work. But if the question is suspended – in the air, almost in the unconscious, to manifest itself later in some way in the interior work or in the work on oneself during the rehearsals – I don't react against this. In this case the question outlines itself, but is not formulated, not even in thought. The moment in which it becomes formulated is very dangerous, because it can transform the thing into an alibi to justify the lack of quality of the performance. To think: "I will do a performance which is the 'work on oneself,'" can mean in the world as it is: "I have the liberty to not do well my work in the play, because in truth I am looking for other riches." And here we are already at the catastrophe.

IX

Not long ago someone asked me: "Do you want the Center of Grotowski to continue after you disappear?" I responded "no" simply because I responded to the *intention* of the question; it seemed to me the intention was: "Do you want to create a System which stops at the point your research stopped, and that then becomes taught?" To this I responded "no." But I must acknowledge that if the intention had been: "Do you want that this tradition, which in a certain place and a certain time you have reopened, do you want therefore that this *research* on Art as vehicle, that someone continue it?", I would not be able to respond with the word "no."

In our work there is a paradox. We are doing Art as vehicle, which by its very nature is not destined for spectators, and nevertheless dozens of times, we have confronted theatre groups with this work – but above all *without inciting* these groups to abandon Art as presentation: on the contrary, in the perspective that they should continue it. This paradox is merely apparent. It has been able to happen because Art as vehicle poses in practice questions linked to craft as such, legitimate on either extremity of the chain of the performing arts; questions linked to craftsmanship.

At the Workcenter, there exists also an aspect of formation. At the beginning of section V, I pointed out that one pole of work at the Workcenter is tending toward permanent education in the field of acting (even if it is yet related to ritual forms). The young artists, who are at the Workcenter (for a year, and sometimes much longer) and who take part in this pole of work, do it in the perspective of their craft: the craft of the actor, and I use the possibilities of the Workcenter to be a help to them in this field.

133

At the same time, I am not deaf to the question of whether the craft as such cannot suggest something about the work on oneself. But it's an extremely delicate question and I prefer to avoid any indoctrination.

It has been given to me to make appear at the Workcenter the other pole of work which is rooted in Art as vehicle – as a tradition and as a research. This does not include directly all those with whom I work. Concerning the persons directly involved in Art as vehicle, I don't think of them as "actors" but as "doers" (those who do), because their point of reference is not the spectator but the itinerary in verticality.

At the Workcenter, that which goes toward Art as vehicle has been confronted with visiting theatre groups. And even if for some persons there appeared practical conclusions, the limited time of these encounters excluded any eventual supposition that it is a question of "my pupils." With Art as vehicle, we are only one extremity of the long chain and this extremity should remain in contact – in one way or another – with the other extremity, which is Art as presentation. Both of the extremities belong to the same large family. A passage between them should be possible: of the technical discoveries, of the artisanal consciousness . . . It is needed that all this can pass along, if we don't want to be completely cut off from the world. I remember that chapter in the Chinese *I Ching*, the ancient Book of Changes, in which it says that the well can be well-dug and the water inside of it pure, but if no one draws water from this well, the fish will come to live there and the water will spoil.

On the other hand, if we make efforts to exert an influence, there is the danger of mystification. I prefer therefore to not have such pupils who bring the world the Good News. But if there arrives to the others a message of rigor, of exigence which reflects certain laws of the "life in art" – then that is another question. This message can be more transparent than that colored by a missionary task or by an exclusivity of orientation.

In the history of art (and not only of art) we can find innumerable examples of how a *looked for* influence either rapidly dies or transforms itself into a caricature, into a denaturation so radical, that often it is difficult to find in the widespread image even a trace of that which was the source. On the other hand, there exist these anonymous influences. Both extremities of the chain (Art as presentation and Art as vehicle) should exist:

one visible – public – and the other almost invisible. Why do I say "almost"? Because if it were entirely hidden, it could not give life to the anonymous influences. For this, it should remain invisible, but *not entirely*.